Supporting Teacher Development

Supporting Teacher Development

New Skills for Principals in Supervision and Evaluation

Debra Eckerman Pitton

ROWMAN & LITTLEFIELD
Lanham • Boulder • New York • London

Published by Rowman & Littlefield
A wholly owned subsidiary of The Rowman & Littlefield Publishing Group, Inc.
4501 Forbes Boulevard, Suite 200, Lanham, Maryland 20706
www.rowman.com

Unit A, Whitacre Mews, 26-34 Stannary Street, London SE11 4AB

British Library Cataloguing in Publication Information Available

Library of Congress Cataloging-in-Publication Data

ISBN 978-1-4758-2513-8 (cloth : alk. paper) -- ISBN 978-1-4758-2514-5 (pbk. : alk. paper) -- ISBN 978-1-4758-2515-2 (electronic)

∞ ™ The paper used in this publication meets the minimum requirements of American National Standard for Information Sciences Permanence of Paper for Printed Library Materials, ANSI/NISO Z39.48-1992.

Printed in the United States of America

This book is dedicated to my daughter, Laura Pitton Guerrero, a teacher with a loving heart and strong skills who suffered through her own challenging teaching evaluation process. Her enthusiasm for teaching and her efforts to improve and support her students, as well as her effort to overcome an early negative evaluation experience, motivated me to write this text.

Contents

Preface

When I talk with educators about teacher evaluation, no one questions the need for feedback to improve teaching. There is much written about assessment, evaluation, data gathering and analysis related to teaching. The part of teacher evaluation that seems to get overlooked is the human factor. Teachers are not computers or machines that can be "fixed" with mere input from a reviewer.

The human mind and heart have to be considered when providing critical feedback. Most teachers choose to work with young people in schools because they want to make a difference. They care about children and learning and want to do well. So supervisors who have the role of evaluating teachers need to embrace the belief that teachers are "doing good."

Most teachers have areas where they could improve, but principals need to approach the evaluation process with a firm belief that the teacher is working to the best of their ability at this time, to support the learners in their classroom. Principals need to consider how deeply personal the act of teaching is to an individual, and craft language that is supportive and designed to recognize the skills of the teacher.

It seems inconceivable that a principal would intentionally provide evaluation data in ways that would be harmful to a teacher. Yet we often fail to consider the damage feedback can do to a person's confidence and belief in themselves as educators. When administrators take their role as evaluator and wed it with the concept of supporting faculty growth, teachers can absorb feedback more easily.

This book takes concepts that are commonly known and lays them out in a way that provides a clear picture of how to manage teacher evaluations and get the desired results. The text includes opportunities for administrators to practice responses to situations that call for thoughtful communication. Scenarios are given so that principals can reflect and discuss their feedback skills with peers.

The social learning opportunities in this text are intentional, calling for evaluators to work with colleagues to consider ways for strengthening their skills in this critical process of giving feedback. The overall goal of this book is to remind principals and educators in evaluator roles to consider how to best gather and share observational feedback in order to create a positive outcome for everyone involved.

Chapter One

Mentoring Skills for Principals

Supporting Teacher Evaluation and Development

This chapter provides rationale for the use of mentoring skills by principals to support evaluation and teacher growth and provides role definitions for discussions as they begin their work together. Underlying principles of mentoring and the support that can be provided by administrators via the use of these skills are identified, as well as the need for such processes.

Evaluation has always been a part of the educator's vocabulary. Teachers evaluate their students in a variety of ways and use that data to determine how students are achieving. Teachers, too, have always been subject to evaluation. In earlier times, teachers were evaluated on their personal character, and good teaching was often equated to being a good role model for students. Later, checklists and templates identifying the teacher behaviors that were expected in the classroom were developed, and principals observed and rated the effectiveness of teachers based on those behaviors.

Research identifying the impact of teacher on student has shifted the focus of evaluations to the accountability of teachers in relation to their students' achievement. Local control over education has meant that teacher evaluation is the purview of the school principals. In the past, however, due to the numerous duties expected of principals and school administrators, many of these evaluations were superficial and rarely happened after a teacher had received tenure.

In 2011, in conjunction with efforts to reauthorize the ESEA (Elementary and Secondary Education Act), opportunities were created for states to compete for grants to assist them in making changes to their teacher evaluation systems. Under the grant criteria, these evaluation systems needed to include multiple levels of quality, including student achievement data. As a result of

2 *Chapter 1*

these grants, school districts are crafting and implementing new teacher evaluation systems.

In the past, teacher evaluation was primarily focused on new teachers. Many experienced teachers had very few, if any, evaluations following tenure. As a result, the uncertainty surrounding these new evaluations, coupled with the additional focus on the achievement of teachers' students, feels threatening and scary for many educators. There is a lot of anxiety and concern about how these new evaluation tools will be implemented and if the processes will be a fair and reliable measure of teachers' work.

At the 2013 International Teacher Education Conference in Jerusalem, Israel, Dr. D. H. Gitomer, Rose and Nicholas DeMarzo Chair in Education at Rutgers University, spoke about his work developing reliability and validity studies on teacher evaluation tools. His goal is to develop observations that lead to insight about teaching and improved teacher quality.

When Dr. Gitomer asked for audience feedback, several teachers admitted that the idea of these new evaluations made them extremely nervous. Knowing that hearing criticism can shut down a listener's positive responses, participant answers to Dr. Gitomer's talk identified a clear need to support teachers as they learn to "take help" and an even greater need for administrators to learn how to "give help." Dr. Gitomer stated his concern that little had been done to help prepare administrators to effectively use these evaluation tools.

Given the myriad of school settings and populations, it is understandable that teachers might be somewhat wary of any new evaluation systems. In response to this concern, Dr. Gitomer followed up his remarks by saying that new teacher evaluations should lead to supportive action, in particular, the implementation of interactive mentoring processes to help facilitate faculty improvement, with the result being increased student learning.

A shared evaluation process between the teacher and evaluator would reflect Dr. Gitomer's idea of supportive action and help create more supportive systems. However, there has not been much input from teachers in the actual evaluation process historically, nor has there been much focus on student learning. Teachers were able respond to an evaluation after the fact, but they were not usually involved in setting up expectations or the process.

So how do administrators implement a shared, supportive teacher evaluation process? Such evaluations, using student data for teacher improvement, will require that administrators communicate with teachers effectively about student learning. This focus on the communication process is a mentoring and coaching skill that is not currently a major component of most updated teacher evaluation tools or principal training. However, mentoring processes can give principals the skills to support teachers in ways that enable educators to hear a critique and be open to follow-up.

Cognitive coaching is a process well suited to develop the type of mediation principals need to support faculty. This model is designed to capitalize on and enhance teachers' pedagogical proceesses and encourage reflection, goal setting, self-monitoring and self-correcting.[1] Cognitive coaching provides a format that can support administrators who wish to examine and hone mentoring and support skills.

A mentor is defined as a guide who supports someone's learning. The term "mentor" comes from Homer's *Odyssey,* and is the name of a wise and learned man who was given the task of educating the son of Odysseus. A principal is a school leader who is charged with managing the learning of the individuals in a school—both students and teachers. Considering this description, it seems important for principals to develop ways to use evaluation as a positive process for teacher growth by investigating skills traditionally used by mentors.

The intersection of the traditional roles of "principal" and "mentor" provides a new way to foster teacher development. Principals can affirm their teachers and create an environment where everyone believes in the goal of working to improve student learning. Even though using evaluation tools and giving feedback can feel uncomfortable, a principal who works to make the process a learning experience supports teacher growth and student achievement. In light of this concept, it becomes important to provide principals the opporutnity to develop the skills for this new component of their work.

The word "mentor" pops up in many conversations. Famous athletes speak of their coaches as mentors. Business leaders talk about mentoring new hires in the operation of a company. High schools and colleges often place students in apprenticeships with a mentor who is doing the job the young person hopes to have some day. All of these descriptions are appropriate, and they are based on a trusting relationship between two people. However, the word "trust" is not a term usually associated with a teacher's description of their relationship with their principal.

A crucial skill used by mentors is the ability to communicate their belief that a person is capable of moving beyond present challenges and accomplishing great things. For principals, this quality is very important, but often is not considered a leadership characteristic. In this era of new teacher evaluations and the emphasis on a teacher's impact on student learning, good administrators must work to implement mentoring strategies that capitalize on opportunities to affirm the potential of their teachers. And principals must do so in a genuine and caring way that fosters trust.

Leadership studies consistently refer to the need for principals to use effective communication skills when working to advocate for new ideas and persuade faculty to adjust their practice. So, too, with evaluations, administrators need to be transparent about their expectations for teachers and set up goals as well as supports. Research on mind-set, which states that individuals have the power to grow and change and that intelligence is not fixed, is also an important concept for administrators.[2]

In this context, principals who do not hold this belief—that all of their teachers are capable of increasing their knowledge and skills—will have difficulty helping teachers improve. This growth mind-set, a belief in the ability of all teachers to improve, is key for anyone working to support teacher development. A crucial characteristic of mentors is the ability to communicate their belief that a person is capable of transcending present challenges and of accomplishing great things in the future. Principals must "believe" in their teachers.

Considering the pending implementation of updated teacher evaluation processes in most states, it is especially important that principals have the knowledge and tools to support teacher growth. Negative responses to evaluations or processes that are intimidating or punitive will not improve teachers' skills. Administrators who use evaluation tools, expecting improvement in areas identified by the assessment without additional effort on their part, will find little change occurs.

Teacher evaluations must be implemented within an environment of support and learning. Teachers must be given resources and time to practice, to evaluate, to reflect, and to adjust their new skills before being expected to apply them effectively in the classroom.

However, administrators who would like to support teacher development are not usually given enough direction or guidance in this area. This is a critical element—supporting principals as they develop mentoring skills.

This learning process needs to involve more than just knowledge acquisition; principals need a range of mentoring skills to be effective. Experiential learning, the use of active learning that engages the individual, is one of the most effective processes for developing these skills. Because mentoring is a social interaction, learning mentoring skills needs to take place within a social learning context. Active learning, focused on dialogue and conversation, is a necessary and powerful tool for developing principals' effective mentoring skills.

As with any new learning, the opportunity to hear different perspectives, reflect, and rethink is the key to true understanding. Talking to other principals, hearing differing ideas and reflecting are vital to administrators' continued learning and to putting these new skills into practice. When educators have the opportunity to share their experiences or their approaches to new ideas with other educators, what they learn moves beyond a mechanical approach and becomes an embedded, effortless skill.

As principals converse about their efforts to use mentoring practices, integrated, personalized approaches emerge as they make connections between what they know and do and the skill they are working to develop. Utilizing reflective, systematic thinking about mentoring helps principals become better problem solvers who can monitor and adjust their interactions to support faculty learning.

Principals need to learn and practice mentoring skills that use evaluation data to support teachers. However, conversations about evaluation results can be difficult, and the challenges of these discussions reinforce the need to provide support for both teachers and administrators. Before any assistance can be accepted by the teacher, a relationship must be developed between the two individuals.[3] Wise educational leaders will not leave this critical component of relationship building to chance.

Opportunities to collaborate with other administrators in this learning process should be provided to principals. The dialogue and reflection components of mentor skill development need to be available—either through a formal process or by an informal group of principals who work together to enhance their skills. It is highly beneficial if educators studying mentoring processes have another administrator available for feedback. To that end, this text provides opportunities for principals to engage in this type of learning and personal development, either alone or with colleagues.

The use of mentoring or coaching skills can vary from one school district to the next. No matter the district, however, it is important that all individuals involved in these interactions know and understand their roles. This is especially true if a principal is implementing mentoring skills into their faculty interactions. A lack of clarity regarding roles can lead to confusion and ineffective support for teachers.

Considering the possible shift in perception of roles for the teacher and administrator when the principal is using mentoring practices, it is vital that roles be defined. By examining roles in their relationships, teachers and principals can identify their perspectives and discuss ways to come to a shared understanding of these roles. When everyone has a clear picture of what they expect from each other, the relationship can develop into a more effective and supportive process.

The following descriptions will help clarify the roles and can be used as a starting point in discussions among faculty and principals.

The Teacher:

The role of the teacher is to be open to the process, to commit to the relationship, and to continue learning. It is imperative that teachers be open to the idea of receiving input. Although this may seem like an obvious point, if teachers believe that they have the necessary skills to be successful in the classroom, they may feel uncomfortable or even threatened by the idea of a process that provides them with a critique of their work—even if there is the promise of support. Many people prefer to work on their own to enhance their skills. Some approach their teaching with the belief that it is a sign of weakness or failure to accept help.

Educators need to be open to suggestions and support from principals and view their role as that of a partner in strengthening the teaching profession. This is easier for some individuals than for others, but it is critical that teachers recognize this aspect of their role. A willingness to be open to the evaluation process is needed.

Principals can help by discussing the teacher's perception of the process and acknowledging that it is often difficult for people to discuss feedback related to their work. If teachers can identify their concerns about the idea of evaluation, they open the door to the process. By focusing on developing a more open relationship, teachers and principals create an environment that fosters a culture that is receptive to ongoing learning.

Teachers also must be willing to commit to the time it takes to work with someone else. Since many pressures and expectations are placed on teachers, they often consider it easier to work alone rather than to carve out a few minutes to meet with someone to discuss their work. Teachers' commitment to the process, their willingness to join in all of the learning activities and to spend time with their principals and colleagues is a necessary component for a positive relationship and successful evaluation process.

It is also important that the teacher sees his or her role as that of a learner. Becoming a successful teacher is an ongoing process, and the concept of being a lifelong learner should be internalized. New knowledge brought to the evaluation process must be used as a basis for discussion. It is important that principals stress that new understandings do not devalue what has been learned previously but rather extends knowledge in new directions to help meet the needs of students.

If teachers see themselves as lifelong learners, they will be able to weigh new ideas suggested by the principal and consider how these ideas fit with their current teaching philosophies. They will conduct action research to find answers to their questions. They will work with colleagues. They will stretch themselves in new directions. Teachers who want only to keep the tools they already have and not venture in any new directions, do not fulfill their role in the learning relationship.

The Principal:

The role of the principal is that of guide, supporter, and resource (as well as evaluator). As a guide, the principal needs to help teachers negotiate the challenges of addressing the results of an evaluation. Like Socrates, the mentor needs to provide ideas and encouragement to broaden the teachers' repertoire so they extend their skills. It is imperative then, that the evaluation process be framed by a supportive relationship.

This is not an easy task. Principals are responsible for administering teacher evaluations, so they must have a clear sense of the evaluator's role, yet be able to "switch hats" when providing support for teacher growth and become that "guide on the side." In this way, the evaluation process becomes a vehicle for identifying areas where the principal can focus their support to enhance the teacher's development.

In the role of supporter, principals champion teachers' development by seeking ways to support and provide assistance. Considering Dweck's research on mind-set, principals need to focus on teachers' strengths and not begin with a deficit model. As much as possible, evaluations must be framed by the learning and support process, with the evaluation tool used primarily for identifying areas to focus the teacher's learning. As identified by many research studies, confidentiality must be ensured and conversations between the administrator and teacher need to remain private.

Because a social relationship is beneficial when people are engaging in conversations that support teacher learning, principals must be willing to schedule time to connect with teachers in order to get better acquainted. The ability of a principal to interact positively with teachers depends on the strength of their relationship, and effective communication supports the development of the relationship.

Participants in this evolving relationship need to be clear and comfortable with the job-embedded role each person identifies as their own. Administrators and teachers can use the checklists included below to expand their understanding of their roles and develop a shared understanding of expectations within this learning interaction. These checklists can serve as starting points for a discussion of what principals and teachers expect from their interactions.

The following lists were compiled by experienced educators from various school districts and reflect the activities identified as corresponding to each role. Each participant should fill out the checklists for both roles. Participants should feel free to add additional components that are relevant for their particular school's site or position.

After completing both checklists, principals and teachers should discuss and explain their priority rankings and then discuss why they consider an item to be a valid expectation for each role. They need to consider why some aspects of the role rank higher for them than others.The goal is to come to some consensus. In this way, perceptions about the roles and responsibilities for all participants can be identified and discussed.

Teachers should also discuss these roles with colleagues, perhaps in their PLC (professional learning community) meetings, to identify common ground. Principals could gather with other administrators and identify their individual rankings. After discussing their perspectives with colleagues, administrators and faculty should come back together and share the results of these conversations and expand on their choices and rationale regarding these roles within their relationship. This type of dialogue will help define the roles and expectations of everyone involved in the school and create a strong start to the evaluation and learning experience.

EXPECTATIONS FOR THE TEACHER

The following list identifies the expectations for teachers in this learning partnership. Please prioritize the list by scoring each item to reflect the importance of this expectation for you.

1 = critically important; 2 = very important; 3 = somewhat important; 4 = not important

The teacher will:

_____be open to developing a relationship with the principal;

_____ be willing to try new ideas and suggestions offered by the principal;

_____ bring to the experience ideas for topics and subjects that he or she would like to incorporate in his or her teaching;

_____ be willing to discuss their knowledge base and their awareness of district, state and/or national standards;

_____ be willing to work with colleagues to implement new ideas/suggestions;

_____ be willing to expand their students' interactions via discussion groups, cooperative learning lessons, and by engaging students in higher-order questions, projects, and activities;

_____ reshape lesson plans to incorporate varying formats;

_____ reshape and articulate a classroom management plan;

_____ fine-tune lesson plans to add flexibility for change when schedules and student needs dictate;

_____ reshape lesson plans that break down a concept and create a process for teaching it;

_____ identify objectives for the day/lesson in a visual way to share with students;

_____ expand their assessment strategies;

_____ identify his or her own learning style and explore how this learning style impacts his or her teaching;

_____ observe teachers from a variety of subject areas and varying grade levels;

_____ expand lessons to engage students with varying degrees of ability;

_____ participate in the school's learning structure (PLC);

_____ communicate with the administrator in scheduled meetings;

_____ exhibit a strong presence—the ability to communicate positively and professionally in the classroom;

_____ craft lessons that address the various learning styles and multicultural identities of his or her students;

_____ maintain confidentiality;

_____ others? (write in additional components for this role).

EXPECTATIONS FOR THE PRINCIPAL

The following list identifies expectations for the principal in a this evaluation-learning relationship. Please prioritize the list by scoring each item to reflect the importance of this expectation for you.

1 = critically important; 2 = very important; 3 = somewhat important; 4 = not important

The principal will:

_____ communicate his or her expectations and goals for the teacher

_____ allow the teacher to develop his or her own teaching style

_____ arrange for release time to provide learning experiences for the teacher

_____ maintain confidentiality

_____ arrange/encourage observations in other classes, levels of ability, and grade levels

_____ arrange for interactions with the teacher on a regular, informal basis

_____ provide an opportunity and resources for the teacher to videotape his or her teaching both early and late in the semester/year to self-evaluate

_____ provide resources that support and encourage the implementation of a variety of curricular, teaching, and assessment strategies

_____ provide models of how to infuse multiculturalism on a daily basis (beyond the curriculum, as a part of life in the school)

_____ provide models of instruction differentiated for students with varying needs

_____ create a schedule that ensures communication with teachers

_____ provide time for professional development for teachers

_____ model effective interpersonal communication skills

_____ be aware of what is going on in the teacher's classroom by observing on a regular basis using walk-throughs or other models

_____ share observational data that provides evidence of the teacher's classroom interactions and teaching strategies with the teacher

_____ review lesson plans for alignment with standards and teacher goals

_____ review the observational tool (the lens) that will be used for evaluation to be sure teachers have a clear understanding of the expectations embedded in the tool

_____ offer resources in areas requested by the teacher

_____ provide opportunities for all faculty to obtain and share curricular materials

_____ provide a variety of learning opportunities within the school (workshops, professional development, peer observations, etc.)

_____ Work to create an atmosphere of collegiality in the school

_____ others? (write in any additional components for this role that you identify)

NOTES

1. Jackson, Y., and McDermott, V. (2012). Aim High, Achieve More: How to Transform Urban Schools through Fearless Leadership. Alexandria, VA: ASCD, p. 86.

2. Dweck, C. (2006). Mindset: The New Psychology of Success. New York: Ballantine Books.

3. Gold, Y. (1992). Psychological Support for Mentors and Beginning Teachers: A Critical Dimension. In T. Bey and C. Holmes (Eds.), Mentoring: Contemporary Principles and Issues. Reston, VA: Association of Teacher Educators.

Chapter Two

Creating an Environment That Supports Ongoing Teacher Learning

Developing trust is a key element in shaping an environment that enables teachers to respond to evaluation data in positive, productive ways. This chapter identifies the often overlooked need for trust building and offers ways principals can build trusting relationships in a school community. Processes and skills that are a part of developing positive relationships are identified and practice options included.

The stated goal of most principals is to create an environment where students learn successfully. To accomplish this goal, faculty and administration need to collaborate to support the learning of their students. Collaboration works when there is a solid relationship among participants, and yet the relationship among faculty and administrators is not always an important area of focus within a school. Mentoring is a relational skill, and using effective mentoring processes can assist a principal as he or she works to develop positive relationships with staff.

Positive interactions between principals and faculty, like all relationships, need to be based on trust. Administrators can be seen as "the opposition" by some faculty, because the principal is the person who has to set budgets, make decisions about resources, enforce policies and hire, and evaluate staff. When an administrator's goal is to mentor and support faculty, there has to be trust established, or these negative perceptions might surface.

Without trust, it is difficult for faculty to be sure of the administrator's motives and as a result, teachers may approach conversations warily. Trust is vital to achieving the goal of supporting teachers with their ongoing growth and development. It is easy for someone to say, "Trust me." However, the words must be backed up by actions and statements that prove the trust is warranted.

When teachers are working with a principal whom they don't know very well, trust is not yet established. Researchers specifically state that school leaders need to have the trust of their faculty and staff to be effective.[1] The administrator may want to establish trust, but it is not automatic; it takes time to develop. It is imperative that administrators make time available to build trust with their teachers at the start of their relationship, when they join the faculty, or when the principal begins a new position with a school.

Trust is created by communication that is frequent, clear, and honest. Principals need to use the first days of the school year to schedule meetings where they can begin to start the trust-building process. Administrators need to provide the time for trust building, because without a commitment of time, a trusting relationship will not develop. Principals who want to enable their faculty to hear and respond positively to evaluations need to recognize that it will take time to create an environment of trust.

To be effective, principals need to be committed to doing whatever it takes to help teachers be successful, including focusing administrative time and energy on relationship building. Once administrators have determined that they are comfortable with the time commitment required for this component of their work, initial interactions with teachers need to focus on building a trusting relationship. From the very first meeting, they must show themselves to be available and empathetic.

One way to demonstrate these qualities is to share ideas and experiences. Without sharing, there is no relationship. Principals who take the time to meet with faculty in small groups (departments), professional learning groups, or one-on-one, will find it easier to create a positive, trusting environment. These connections need to happen before in-depth conversations about evaluation can occur. Principals should begin by talking about experiences, hobbies, and leisure activities to allow themselves to get to know the faculty (and vice versa) beyond their specific role in the school.

This first step in developing trusting relationships requires self-disclosure. Administrators who share information about themselves usually find that their level of intimacy is reciprocated. When people share information about themselves, the listener usually responds in kind. This is an important insight for principals. It can be challenging to draw the line between personal and professional relationships, but administrators who want to get to know their faculty on a more personal basis in order to build trust, need to share some of themselves.

Principals often refrain from self-disclosure because they feel uncomfortable projecting a "too familiar" image. However, trust develops when one takes a risk and discloses a thought or feeling, and the other person responds. When sharing stories and information becomes more comfortable and natural, the listener (teacher) is more likely to trust the principal. Administrators who are self-deprecating and humble in their interactions with their teachers communicate that as principals, they do not know everything, and that they are also still learning. This communication process builds trust.

Faculty members are more apt to see administrators as supporters when principals honestly share their own fears and concerns. Without such disclosure by administrators, it is unlikely that faculty will feel they can share their feelings or concerns, or be open about their weakness or struggles in the classroom. Reciprocal sharing, starting with safe topics and building up to more difficult issues, is the path to building trust. If teachers are going to trust that the principal is truly concerned with the teachers' growth and development, and not "out to get them"—there must be trust.

The challenges of building trust and mentoring effectively are magnified in cross-cultural situations. Stereotypes may influence perceptions of behavior and communication style when educators, who bring with them very different background experiences, work together. Administrators need to consider that their behaviors may be overlaid with issues of power, historical tensions, and institutional racism. Therefore, it is imperative that ongoing discussions about gender, race, and racism between faculty and administrators be honest and open.

Self-disclosure can be especially challenging when an individual is unsure of how their story will be accepted. When sharing an experience that is radically different from that of the administrator, teachers need to be heard and have their experience validated. Administrators need to "match the message to the listener" in order to structure conversation in a meaningful way.

Teachers and principals from diverse backgrounds need to be aware of their own perspectives and biases. They need to be open to the stories of others that may be very different from their own experiences. Discounting or ignoring the influence of individuals' life stories can negatively impact the development of any type of supportive relationship. Below is a scenario for principals to read and reflect upon. This dialogue provides a brief example of an initial conversation with a new faculty member.

Consider how this conversation might be an example of a trust-building situation. Try role-playing with a colleague, using this situation or your own ideas, and reflect on how this initial exchange plays out. Paying deliberate attention to establishing and conducting initial trust-building conversations using self-disclosure can help administrators develop positive relationships and a supportive environment in their school.

SCENARIO FOR TRUST BUILDING: INITIAL DISCLOSURE

Role-play and analyze this initial conversation on your own or with another administrator or colleague. While reading this sample dialogue, look for signs of trust building and think about what else you notice in the principal's choice of conversation.

> **Principal:** (shakes hands) Hi, _____! I am glad to get a chance to chat with you. Thanks for letting me drop in this morning before classes start. Would you like some coffee? I brought some from the teacher's lounge—I don't know about you, but I need to begin my day with coffee.

> **Teacher:** (taking the coffee) Thanks.

> **Principal:** I thought we could take a few minutes to talk about the school and the neighborhood. I know you are one of our experienced teachers and I am excited to join you and the other teachers here at (name of school). I'd love to know how you have seen the school evolve since you arrived.

> **Teacher:** Well, the demographics have changed, that's for sure. We have more challenges than we did ten years ago.

> **Principal:** (nodding her head a bit in agreement). I find that adjusting to changes is something I really have to work at. When I moved to a seventh grade teaching position, I had never taught in a midde school, only at a high school, and adjusting to the kids' energy level took me a while.

> **Teacher:** Well you will have fun adjusting to the changes in the community here!

> **Principal:** What are some of those changes?

> **Teacher:** We don't have the kids from the neighbohood anymore. The new district busing system brings students in from all over, and we just don't have the same connection with them.

> **Principal:** It is hard when you don't feel connected to a community—I am feeling a bit that way now as the new person here. I'd like to hear some more of your insights into the changes that have occurred here—maybe we can talk again later?

> **Teacher:** Sure.

Debrief with a partner regarding the conversation or write down your thoughts about these questions.

- What did you hear in this initial conversation?
- How did the principal try to establish a trusting relationship?

- What would you talk about next?
- Did you hear any examples of self-disclosure? If so, describe the example and identify how it was/was not matched by the listener.

After sharing thoughts or jotting down ideas, principals should consider whether their thoughts were similar to those of their colleagues. Reflect on how you felt and how your colleague perceived the interaction. Previously, principals who have reviewed this dialogue identified comments/actions that are welcoming (Would you like some coffee?); self-disclosing ("I had trouble adjusting to seventh grade energy levels." "Change is hard."); empathetic ("It can be hard when you feel disconnected."); sharing of feelings ("I'm feeling that way now.") and rapport building ("I'd like to hear your insights.")

These comments, statements, and questions are designed to start building a trusting relationship. When these conversations come naturally, it is more comfortable for the principal and teacher. But like any skill, practicing trust-building conversations is important. Trying out the language with the intent to create rapport and self-disclose will enable the administrator to develop more natural, personal conversations in the future. Engaging in practice conversations with purposeful intent is necessary and helpful, but reflecting on the process is the key to growth. Administrators can use the following questions and comments as conversation starters to practice their relationship-building skills.

- What do you like to do on the weekends? Do you play golf/tennis/etc.? (Name other faculty they might be able to connect with who also play a sport.)
- I am tired of the places where I go when I eat out. Do you have any suggestions? What kind of restaurants do you prefer?
- Have you had a chance to travel much? I really want to go to _____.

Principals should try to share some of their own personal experiences during an the initial conversation, such as a difficult situation they experienced as a first year teacher, or a challenging aspect of a past parent conference.

Avoid having teachers come to your office for a conversation—it may not feel comfortable when you have been "called into the principal's office." Go to the teachers' space to have these conversations. The environment makes a difference. Go to the teacher's classroom or to a grade-level or department meeting where you are in the teachers' space. Be present and available for converstions in the halls and at PLC meetings and faculty development sessions. This equalizes the conversation a bit and helps further develop the relationship.

To avoid initial conversations that take on the tone of an interview—or, worse, an interrogation—principals can lead into the conversation using a connection to their own lives. For example, an administrator might preface the question about leisure time by saying, "I really enjoyed this summer (or the weekend, or a holiday). I was able to do _____, which I really like. What do you do when you have free time?"

Prefacing statements in this way allows the conversation to flow more naturally. If administrators reveal something about themselves before asking a question, they create a personal connection with the teacher they are chatting with.

Early on in the developing relationship, it is also important for principals to initiate a discussion about the roles of the administrator and faculty member, as described in chapter 1. This is a more formal approach to creating a supportive environment, and before beginning these activities, the principal needs to frame the discussion/activity and identify the purpose: to intentionally build positive connections between and among faculty and administration.

The administrator and faculty members need to be clear about their roles. Teachers need to know the parameters of these relationships and what the expectations are for how the various members of the faculty, PLC, team of teachers, and administrator in that school will work together.

Another more defined process that administrators might use for building relationships is a metaphor exchange. Principals can use metaphors to describe their vision of teaching and use this metaphor to structure initial discussions once they get beyond introductory conversations. This is another more formal conversation that needs to be framed for participants. Why are you doing this? What is the purpose? Answer these questions to clarify that the discussion is a way to share perspectives.

A discussion using metaphors can be a part of a faculty meeting and can set a base for future conversations. An exchange of metaphors provides a means of sharing views of teaching. It is important that administrators not assign any negative value to a teacher's metaphor/vision of teaching or to the way he or she defines the roles of teacher and administrator. Instead, teachers and administrators need to discuss the similarities and differences in their perspectives to identify what is held in common.

Being aware of another's perspectives gives the relationship a starting point to build on and helps foster a trusting relationship. This honest sharing—removed from any talk about specific problems or the evaluation process, lays the groundwork for future conversations that may focus on more challenging topics.

There are as many different styles of teaching as there are teachers, and it is important that both principals and teachers find a way to describe their personal view of the profession prior to beginning a dialogue about evaluation. Our vision of our work guides our actions. When individuals define their vision of teaching explicitly, it becomes easier for them to articulate their educational perspective and philosophy.

Through such discussions, principals and teachers can come to a shared understanding of what teaching is all about for each person. A dialogue like this allows individuals to more readily understand how a teacher views their work and sets the stage for discussions of where to go next. The use of metaphors is a simple, yet powerful way to describe teaching. By using this literary device to synthesize their view of teaching, teachers can visualize their approach to the classroom and share it with others.

For example, one high school teacher uses the metaphor of an orchestra conductor as an illustration of her vision of teaching. "Each group of players (students) play from the same score, but they all play different parts, like instruments. When all of the parts are added together, they create a whole, beautiful, musical piece of learning." This teacher is describing her work to meet the needs of a variety of learners while striving to help them all succeed. Thus, the metaphor of an orchestra conductor works well as a descriptor of this individual's teaching and helps articulate a vision of her work with students.

Because metaphors and similes provide opportunities for principals to begin sharing their vision of teaching without preaching or lecturing, the following activity can help teachers and administrators structure this process and explore their visions of teaching.

Using imagey to describe teaching:

1. Compare the metaphor of the conductor described above with the following two metaphors shared by teachers. What do these images say about the teachers' views of teaching?

   a. "I see teaching as mountain climbing. As the teacher, I lead the climbers. I struggle to move up the mountain of learning step by step; and after I have made it, I turn and grasp the hands of my students, pulling them up behind me."
   b. "As the teacher, I am a fountain showering my students with all they need to know to be successful in my class."

What does each metaphor say about the teacher? What insights might these descriptions give you about each person?

2. Develop a metaphor or simile to describe your vision of teaching. Brainstorm about the various aspects of your work and take notice of what images come to mind when you think about teaching. Avoid using examples you have heard and develop one that identifies a unique image of your own philosophy of teaching. Use visuals as well as words to create this metaphor.

An opportunity for a faculty to create and draw their image of teaching can be an interesting starting point for conversations about teaching and learning. Everyone can engage in the activity as a means of fostering a shared understanding of one another's views of teaching. The principal should let the faculty know that he or she has a metaphor for teaching as well; however, the principal should wait to share their image. Waiting to share their vision will encourage faculty to be more open, as opposed to perhaps just reacting to the principal's metaphor.

Directions:

1. Create a verbal and visual metaphor or simile that reflects your beliefs about teaching (Teaching is . . .) or a simile (Teaching is like . . .)
2. Prepare to share your metaphor with colleagues.
3. First, simply show the image to a colleague and ask them to let you know what the metaphor says to them.
4. Follow up with your own comments. Did your metaphor reflect who you are and/or your vision of teaching? Did your partner understand your imagery?
5. Switch roles and have your partner share their metaphor.
6. Conclude with a discussion about the similarities and differences between your methapor and your partner's. Do you find some references to your own beliefs reflected your partner's views on teaching and learning as well?
7. Finally, after all pairs have had their exchanges, ask for individuals to volunteer to share with the entire group or PLC.
8. Finish with the principal sharing his or her metaphor and asking for input from the faculty regarding its meaning.

This metaphor exercise provides principals with a process that enables them to define their own vision of teaching as well as develop an understanding of faculty members' visions of teaching and learning. The sharing of this understanding is another first step in relationship development. Without such a dialogue, administrators might view what is going on in faculty classrooms only through their own perspective.

Dialogue about personal views on teaching enable individuals an opportunity to compare their own vision of teaching with others, gaining them insight into the similarities and differences in their thinking. Likewise, it is important that principals understand their teachers' views and how those perspectives influence their classroom practices and interactions.

With this understanding, principals can support the kind of learning that helps teachers maintain their vision, but perhaps extend it in new ways. In addition, the administrator gains insights that can help frame evaluation data at a later date and provide a deeper understanding of particular teachers' thinking. Knowing more about a teacher's vision of their work provides insights so administrators can help move faculty toward higher levels of teaching in the future.

Following this activity, administrators also can help foster a new understanding of what teaching should be. However, unless both parties are very clear on how they view teaching and learning at that point in time, miscommunication and misunderstanding will occur. The principal should remember that the teacher's view is his or her reality and must be considered in all conversations about teaching. It is important to know where teachers are regarding their vision of teaching, so principals' next steps can respond to the teachers' perspective.

When a principal understands the faculty's vision of teaching, the metaphors can be used to consider the next steps. Perhaps faculty members might group themselves according to similarities in their visions; perhaps they might discuss the differences in their vision and what reasons support their perspectives. With this activity, principals have a starting point to reinforce common views of teaching and learning or to begin to stretch teacher thinking regarding their views.

Modeling of classroom interactions that demonstrate alternative perspectives might be a follow-up. Administrators can provide a demonstration of a new strategy or skill and ask teachers to reflect on how they view the demonstrated method. Through this modeling-reflection process, an educator's vision can be influenced to incorporate additional understandings of the teaching and learning processes and help set up a willingness to continue to be open to new ideas.

If an administrator facilitates a metaphor discussion and provides modeling of new or alternative teaching strategies prior to evaluation discussions or implementation of teacher observations, it can lay the groundwork for addressing new ideas, without the fear of being "graded" or "scored" by an evaluation. It is important for principals to acknowledge that what is being modeled may not yet be in everyone's vision of teaching, but that this is perhaps a new concept to be discussed and considered.

After conducting the initial metaphor sharing and some follow-up activities, principals still need to continue developing their relationships with teachers. At a later faculty meeting, the administrator could reintroduce the metaphor activity and ask teachers to share any new comments about their metaphor, or talk about any additions or changes they would make to their vision at this point in time.

Questions about how the earlier modeled lesson might fit with their metaphor could be asked. This is an opportunity to discuss how teachers are working to actualize the metaphors they created, or perhaps identify if their metaphor is changing. If teachers want to rewrite their metaphors, principals can discuss how they might focus their learning to support their revised visions of teaching. Administrators can help reaffirm original metaphors or help develop new metaphors that reflect newly discovered, but positive, visions of teaching.

Principals may need to adjust their own visions of teaching after working with faculty on this learning activity. It is not uncommon to hear about mentors who describe the profound positive effect their protégées had on their own perspectives. The same is true for principals working to develop these mentoring skills. Administrators might discover that their own perspectives have been reshaped through conversations and new relationships with faculty.

Teachers and administrators should "check signals" every now and then to make sure perspectives of each are still relevant and understood. If a vision is renewed or rewritten, discussion of the changes and support for this new vision of teaching should be encouraged. "Checking signals" is a process where the principal informally asks if people want to revisit their earlier discussion on metaphors, or add to it.

After working with the faculty on the metaphor-sharing and modeling activities, administrators should share any insights they have had regarding their own vision of teaching. It is another opportunity for self-disclosure, regarding the principal's own learning, and serves as another step in developing the relationship and building the trust needed to facilitate effective evaluations in the future.

NOTE

1. Marzano, R., and Toth, M. (2013). *Teacher Evaluation That Makes a Difference.* Alexandria, VA: ASCD.

Chapter Three

Effective Communication

Making Sure You Can Be Heard

This chapter focuses on effective communication and practice scenarios that support the development of honest and open communication. While talking is a common process, effective communication is not so common, and miscommunication can create barriers that impede teacher development. A review of processes that facilitate positive interactions and opportunities to practice these skills are incorporated into this chapter.

Trust is created by communication that is frequent, clear, and honest. This open communication process is necessary to build trust, and trust is necessary for open communication. This endless loop makes it difficult for principals to know where to begin their focus. It is important that they remember that this process is not linear, but circular, so a starting point is needed. If an administrator wants effective communication to be a part of what occurs in their school, then they need to be the one to initiate it.

Relationship development requires that principals spend time communicating with faculty—getting to know them, listening to what they have to say and considering their feelings and goals. This process needs time before administrators move to more substantive discussions. Leadership relies on effective communication, and good principals regularly and intentionally utilize communication skills to create a positive environment and improve what happens in their schools.

Principals can more effectively communicate openly and build trust if they put some thought and effort into this process. As humans, we talk all the time, so it is easy to forget to take the time to be planful and to communicate thoughtfully. Administrators need to carefully consider the best way to get their ideas and suggestions across to faculty.

To facilitate positive communication, some conversation guidelines should be established for interactions. While it may not seem necessary to establish guidelines for principal/teacher discussions, communication conflicts can be avoided by having a plan for approaching conversations, in particular, conversations about teacher evaluations. Principals can use the guidelines identified below or create their own to fit the needs of their particular institution. The best situation would be to generate communication guidelines with the faculty.

These conversation guidelines will be a starting point for developing trust and open communication.Without a clear focus on communication and the creation of an open process, teachers will not be able to "hear" feedback shared by a principal from an evaluation tool. There are too many emotions and personal self-confidence issues that suface during evaluations for teachers to be able to take in and process comments from anyone they do not trust.

It is vital to have had some previous open communication interactions between the principal and teacher prior to a discussion about evaluation. Administrators who work on this communicative process together with their faculty can enhance the effectiveness of their discussions and create a relationship that supports teacher development.

EXAMPLE OF A CONVERSATION GUIDELINE DOCUMENT

The following are the guidelines for conversations between _____
    (name of administrator) and _____ (name of teacher) or the faculty of _____ school.

We agree to:

1. Confidentiality and honesty. We will say what we are thinking and feeling when we talk to each other, knowing that everything we say in one-on-one conversations will be held in strict confidence.

2. Be thoughtful about our choice of language and tone to communicate effectively and graciously.

3. Ask questions. If we are not sure about what has been said, we will ask, "What do you mean?" We will avoid filling in the blanks with our own interpretation—we will check signals and ask for clarification.

4. Create and stick to a schedule. We acknowledge that regular, planned times for discussion, observation/evaluation as well as informal conversations are vital to developing a trusting working relationship. If we have

trouble connecting, we will set up a time for a phone call or conference to discuss any issue, and we will follow up on all concerns in a timely fashion.

5. Respect each other's needs and communication style. We will facilitate this by sharing our own perspectives on communication needs and style, and respect one another's views. For example, it is okay to say that the timing of an unplanned conversation is not the best or that we are uncomfortable with some aspect of a discussion.

6. Guidelines and processes apply to both parties.

7. Others???? _____

Signed by: _____ (principal) and _____ (name of teacher/s) Date: _____

Conversation guides state publicly what both parties agree to do within the context of the relationship. The commitment to this statement provides a base from which trust can be developed, and open communication can occur. One expectation that should be included in all conversation guides is confidentiality. Without an initial agreement that all one-on-one comments, observations, and discussions are confidential, the relationship cannot develop. Trust will evolve more quickly if a commitment is made regarding the privacy of conversations.

This holds for all discussions relating to evaluations and the work individual teachers will be doing in preparation for, and in response to, the evaluation process. Administrators who want to mentor teachers and support work that will enhance and improve a teacher's knowledge and skills, must hold conversations about the teacher's evaluation in confidence. This means administrators cannot share with other faculty members, administrators, or parents any specifics about a teachers' work and goals.

If there are district requirements that identify situations (such as child endangerment) where confidentiality will not be held, these situations need to be specifically identified ahead of time so that the parameters for confidentiality (or openness) are clear. Some individuals find that establishing confidentiality with their principal to be at cross-purposes with what they perceive as the role of an administrator. However, discussions related to a faculty member's teaching skill development needs to be between the two people involved.

Confidentiality ensures that early observations, walk-throughs and formative evaluation conversations are only shared between the principal and the teacher. Other mentors might be involved in the school's support system, and they, too, must observe confidentiality. This creates a safety zone that will help these discussions be productive steps in the teachers's ongoing learning. Discussion of early observations and the resulting actions that the teacher will take to continue their growth are confidential conversations between the administrator and the teacher.

Summative evaluations usually produce data that may become a part of a teacher's personnel file. Data from formal evaluation processes may be available to identified individuals who are involved in the hiring or retaining of teachers, but should go nowhere else. Individuals, such as school board members, who may need to have knowledge of why a particular teacher is retained or let go, need to receive this information in closed, confidential sessions.

Teachers who do not trust that conversations about any of their formative or summative evaluations will be held in confidence by the principal or evaluator will not respond well to requests for action, ongoing learning, or development steps. Clearly naming the process—how many observations and discussions prior to the final evaluation will be held, who has access to the summative data, and so on, ensures that everyone knows and clearly separates the informal and formative discussions from the final summative evaluation.

The framing of this process is important as it helps mitigate any negative experiences that faculty may have had related to evaluation. To move forward and create a supportive process, principals need to clearly articulate and follow their established ground rules in order to generate a positive environment and an engaged school community.

Sometimes it is helpful to just "name the elephant in the room." What is it that keeps individuals from "hearing" constructive comments and feedback? What is it that creates a "block" that prohibits the feedback from being valued and the suggestions implemented?

Trust is certainly a part of this equation; teachers need to trust that when comments are given, the critique is not an indictment of them as individuals, but honestly meant to provide a means of growth. Asking faculty (anonymously) to list the factors that inhibit their use of open communication with their principal can be another valuable tool in supporting and mentoring teachers. Using brief, open-ended questions, such as the following, to elicit faculty response can provide insights for administrators.

Questions for faculty feedback on evaluation conversations

1. How do you feel when you know you are going to receive feedback from your principal?
2. Where does your mind go when you are listening to feedback? Is your reaction different for supportive versus critical comments?

3. What barriers do you think impede your ability to listen to or hear feedback?
4. What would help you "hear" constructive feedback in a more positive way?

Principals can use the information gathered from this survey to continue work on creating a trusting environment and building relationships. A discussion of the responses to this brief survey in a PLC can help a principal become aware of inhibitors he or she may be inadvertently creating, or identify perceptions that faculty carry from earlier interactions with current or former administrators. Honestly addressing the emotional component of hearing feedback enables faculty and administrators to consider how best to shape feedback in supportive ways and to enhance positive communication.

During the getting-acquainted process of relationship development, and particularly in a cross-cultural relationship, it is critical that both parties talk about how they communicate and include any personal or cultural communication perspectives or styles in their conversation guides. For example, during an initial conversation, principals should ask teachers to share their preferences regarding communication. Administrators also need to identify and share their own preferences and styles related to communication.

A principal might say, "I really find that I like to think about an issue for a while before I am ready to decide what to do. I know that some of my colleagues like to jump right in with solutions, but I like to mull things over. So, I may be very quiet about things while I am thinking. This doesn't mean that I am not happy about what I have observed or what we are discussing related to your work, it just means I am thinking. I wanted you to know that so you can get a sense of my communication style. What about you? How do you like to approach issues?"

Administrators need to self-evaluate and describe their own communication style honestly. For example, if they tend to speak loudly and authoritatively, or are impatient when spending a lot of time hashing over details, they should make this aspect of their style clear. Most importantly, principals need to acknowledge that they are continually working to create an inviting communication style.

Following this activity, the administrator should ask about the teacher's preferences. Teachers may use or prefer a different communication style, so principals need to set up conversation guides to identify and validate both individuals' preferences. Principals need to take the lead in establishing this pattern of honest and open discussion about communication, involving teachers in the process. In addition, principals need to be open to modifying their "natural" communication style to provide a more supportive language structure.

Principals and educational leaders should also keep in mind that certain patterns of communication have been described as gender related. Often when men respond to a problem, they include specific ideas for solving the issue, while women lean more toward nurturing and empathetic statements. These particular communication behaviors need to be explored by the principal and faculty to determine if they reflect their own style.

Key elements in the definition of open communication are honesty and trust, but the use of verbal, nonverbal, and paralinguistic interactions must also be considered. Teachers sense that their principals are truthful (or not) from the administrator's words (verbal), their physical expressions and body language (nonverbal), and the tone and inflection of their voice (paralinguistic).

Messages are sent when individuals communicate, but the meaning of these messages is only perceived in the mind of the individual who is receiving them. We all hear things differently. While no administrator intentionally sends mixed signals, if insufficient attention is paid to the use of verbal, nonverbal, and paralinguistic messages, miscommunication results.

Educators also need to be aware that nonverbal communication often contains culturally sensitive components: the distance a person stands from another when speaking, their eye contact, the way individuals take turns talking, how they listen, and when they choose to communicate. When cultural backgrounds differ, it is vital that the principal think carefully about these differences and identify ways to communicate openly with all faculty members.

VERBAL MESSAGES

Verbal messages are often considered to be the most reliable part of a dialogue. Yet if this is so, why is it that spoken words are often misinterpreted? The reason is that people cannot be 100 percent sure that the verbal messages they send are actually what is heard by the listener.

A wife, for example, may check signals sent by her husband on the amount of gas left in their car before using it. If she hears, "There is enough gas to get you there," she may think she has at least a quarter of a tank. If, after hearing this from her husband many times, she has consistently found the needle on the gas gauge to be near empty, she may feel that her husband is not giving her a straight answer. According to his view, however, he is telling her the truth. He believes that even if the gas gauge is near empty, there is enough gas to get her where she wants to go.

The wife does not have the same interpretation of how much gas is "enough." The word "enough" can have a different meaning for individuals.

Over time, this couple will come to understand that "there is enough gas in the car" means one thing to the wife and another to the husband.

Their awareness of the difference in meanings should enable them to prevent conflict. To facilitate this, the wife might ask a more specific question, such as, "Is there at least a half tank of gas left?" She will get a clearer answer because she has asked a more specific question. Individuals in any relationship need to carefully check signals to be sure that what is said has a similar meaning or interpretation for both parties.

Read the following conversation and consider if there is potential for misinterpretation:

Principal: Hi, Sam. I found it really interesting observing you in class today. I'm glad we can take some time to discuss what went on.

Sam: Yeah, things didn't go exactly as I had planned.

Principal: Let's talk about that. What did you plan and how did the actual lesson vary from that plan?

Sam: My goal was to have the kids explore the various properties of paper by having them feel the paper, write on it, tear it, and soak it in water—and I had a whole bunch of different types of paper for them to use. I had wax paper, construction paper, cardboard, typing paper, notebook paper, toilet paper, and paper towels.

Principal: There was a lot for them to explore.

Sam: Yeah—maybe too much. They were so busy doing the tearing and soaking that they didn't write down any of their discoveries.

Principal: I didn't hear any of the directions you gave the students.

Sam: Well, it was a discovery lesson. I didn't want to be too directive. I told them to investigate the properties of the paper and suggested that they feel it, tear it, and soak it in water.

Principal: Discovery lesson?

Sam: Yeah, it's supposed to be a higher level thinking activity.

Principal: What do you mean by a "discovery" lesson?

Sam: Well, I saw an example of a similar lesson at a workshop last summer. The students are supposed to do some activities that help them think critically and then determine the properties of the substance. The students do the thinking—the teacher doesn't tell them the answer.

Principal: Do you think that this particular discovery lesson accomplished what you were trying to do?

Sam: I think so.

Principal: Can you share some evidence that all the students were able to discover the properties?

Sam: Well, they were all engaged in the activity . . . they were talking about the results of doing stuff to the paper, so, yeah, I think they did discover the properties. I just need to help them shape their thoughts a bit more and craft their responses in writing with more detail.

Consider the dialogue above. Are there any words or phrases used by the principal that could be misinterpreted? What about the words used by the teacher—could they be misleading or unclear? Try rewriting this dialogue using different word choices to see if you can use language that is clearer. Ask two people to read your dialogue, so you can practice listening to your word choices and their possible interpretations and implications.

Some educators who analyzed this conversation came up with the following suggestions for clarifying the verbal messages:

- Using the word *interesting* to describe the lesson might be interpreted negatively by the teacher. A simple, "thanks for letting me observe in your class today" might be a better beginning, as it does not allow for as much misinterpretation.
- The question "What did you plan . . . ?" may be supportive because it suggests that the teacher actually did have a plan. However, it could also be an indication that the principal did not think there was a plan and so is asking for the teacher to define their plans for the lesson.
- The reaction statement: "Discovery?" might be interpreted as a negative because there is no context given this solo word, except for it being a question. It might indicate this is not something the administrator cares for or is aware of, or it might be interpreted as simply inquisitiveness. In any case, the solo word choice is potentially open to misinterpretation by the teacher.
- The teacher's statement, "Well, it was a discovery lesson," seems to be justifying the decision or defending it—but without much context. It seems as if the teacher expects the administrator to recognize the process of discovery, and if not, clarification may be needed.

Regardless of your analysis, this role-play demonstrates that administrators and teachers need to think about their word choices to make sure the words are not being misconstrued. For example, to clarify the meaning after saying "interesting," the mentor might have said, "I am always amazed by all the various methods that can be used in the classroom." This extention to the statement could help avoid misinterpretation.

Recent studies suggest that administrators should be careful of the verbs they use, as the verb leads into and "drives" all following words.[1] Thinking and planning ahead of time about the message and carefully considering the verb choices being used can help shape clear communication.

For example, think about how strong you want your message to be. If you intend to be directive, use verbs like "require" or "must do," which are more commanding. If you are trying to leave options open for your listener, you might use verbs like, "suggest" or "should do." While not all conversations can be pre-planned, principals who take the time to think about their word choices and the verbs driving their messages can create more positive interactions.

AVOIDING MISUNDERSTANDINGS

There is no way for individuals to be absolutely sure that what they say is interpreted exactly as intended. It is important that principals check signals by asking questions when they are not sure about what they have heard, or if they wonder how their message was received. It is important that they are sure their words are perceived the way they intended. If administrators think they might have heard something incorrectly, they need to ask, "So you are saying that . . . ?" or "Do you mean . . . ?" to check the accuracy of their interpretation.

Without checking signals about what they heard, principals may have a false impression of what occurred in a classroom or an inaccurate view of what teachers think. If the relationship has a solid foundation based on trust, it is easier for teachers to reciprocate and ask questions for clarification as well.

Another way principals can avoid misinterpretation is to give the lead in conversations to the teacher. For example, when first talking about a classroom visit, the evaluator should not immediately identify what they have observed. They can say, "Thanks for giving me the opportunity to see students in action" or "I appreciate you letting me spend time in your class."

Teachers are usually eager to know if principals approve of a lesson or not; thus, initial comments may be interpreted as approval or disapproval. An administrator's lead-in statement should not indicate feelings or opinions. Lead-in statements should be nonjudgmental and emotionally neutral so that observers do not inadvertently send a signal that interferes with the discussion that follows. If teachers immediately think the principal has concerns about the lesson, the teacher may become defensive and unable to hear comments and suggestions.

On the other hand, if teachers think the principal really liked the lesson, they may discount suggestions for improvement. Statements such as, "That was a complex lesson," "That was nice," or "Wow, I'd be worn out after that class," are vague and can be misinterpreted by an anxious educator. It is easy to imagine a teacher thinking, "A "complex" lesson? What does that mean? Was it too much for the students to do? Is she saying "complex" because I didn't explain things well and she doesn't want to be critical? Was it "complex" because it was confusing?"

A neutral lead-in serves as a transition from the observation to the conversation about the lesson. Ask the teacher for their thoughts on the lesson after thanking them for allowing you to observe. Give the teacher the lead in the first part of the discussion. Try to let the conversation evolve from the teacher's initial comments.

As administrators and teachers work at open communication, conversation guides are useful tools for both to refer to as they check for clarity. If conversation guides are established that indicate both people will work to be open and honest with each other and that they both need to clarify if something is confusing, a reference point for checking signals is established.

Principals can work toward open communication by saying, "In our conversation guide we agreed to be open with each other. So, I would really like it if you would let me know if there is anything I said that is confusing to you or that doesn't seem to connect with what you are thinking about the lesson."

Principals can further investigate the importance of checking signals through the following exercise that focuses on language use.

Dialogue: Exact Language

Ask another administrator (or a family member or a friend) to identify what they mean when they say the following statements and then answer the questions yourself.

Directions: Write down what you mean when you say these phrases (be as specific as possible).

"I'll be there in a few minutes."
"Can I borrow a couple of bucks?"
"What do you think?"
"Come here a second."
"I'll be right there."
"It needs some work."

"It's okay."
"Lots of times."

When you use these words, what do they mean to you?

Sometimes
Always
Never
Usually
Maybe

Next, share your interpretations with each other. What did you learn about yourself and the person you exchanged lists with regarding your understanding of the words? How can you use this knowledge in your work with your teachers?

A person can never be sure about what idea or thought is triggered by specific language. The words "teacher training" conjure up an image for some educators of "teaching dogs new tricks" or suggest that the teacher needs improvement. These words might imply to some listeners that they are not effective or knowledgeable and that they need to be "trained" or "fixed" in some way.

Phrases like "teacher development" or "teacher support" can produce similar images in teachers' minds. Because of this, administrators need to consider their language choices carefully, ask what terminology is preferred, and explain their own use of particular terms and the intended meaning of the words.

The previous exercise demonstrated how important it is to use exact language to help avoid misinterpretation. If, for example, a principal states that a teacher never gets the students refocused after a disruption, this imprecise language may create a barrier, as the teacher might think, "It's not true that I *never* get the students refocused." The principal might have used *never* for impact or just failed to consider how the word might be interpreted. "That was good," "I liked that," and "That needs some work" all are examples of imprecise language.

Administrators can prevent misinterpretation by saying specifically what was good, identifying exactly what occurred in the classroom that they liked and why, and stating what still needs further development. Specific language is much more accurate and effective. Using specific language for feedback that is directly related to the work being discussed is an effective practice. Principals who model and discuss this process can provide ongoing learning for their teachers and themselves.

NONVERBAL MESSAGES

Many people have probably heard the statement, "It's not what you said, it's how you said it." This comment exemplifies how the nonverbal components of communication must be considered as well as the verbal. Nonverbal signals include facial expressions, vocal tone, inflection, and body stance. It is important that nonverbal messages match verbal messages, as people often tend to pay more attention to these signals than to the words.

People's faces and bodies often reveal what they are feeling, even if their words do not. If someone frowns as she tells her guest that she is glad he dropped by to visit, the guest gets the message that the host is really not very pleased that they are visiting. If a person lowers his eyes and looks away as he tells a colleague that he likes her idea, the listener may get the message that the speaker is not sincere. Listeners add meaning to the messages they hear as they make sense of the words and interpret nonverbal signals.

The concept of negative affect reciprocity, when one person's negative behavior generates another's negative behavior, can result from lack of positive or clear, nonverbal communication.[2] Administrators do not want to perpetuate poor communication and misunderstandings by using unclear or inconsistent nonverbal messages.

Sending contradicting verbal and nonverbal signals is a common cause of miscommunication and can create negative reciprocity. People tend to imitate or send back messages they are given in a conversation. If principals want honest conversation, they need to be sure that the listener "sees" and "hears" honesty in what is being said. Administrators can communicate accurately and facilitate more positive conversations if they develop an acute awareness of the following aspects of nonverbal messages.

Body Language and Facial Expressions

The physical components used while speaking are important aspects of nonverbal communication. Usually a person's stance and the way they configure their face while speaking reflects the emotion being communicated. There are physical representations of emotions that are commonly "read" by the person receiving a message.

When a person's face and/or body stance is not reflective of the emotion that they intend to communicate in their message, misunderstanding occurs. Individuals view the way a person's face looks and the way they sit or stand as confirmation of whether the emotion presented via the language is "true."

Not all individuals recognize the nonverbal cues that are commonly associated with particular emotions in our country. Because individuals may misread the physical representation of an emotion expressed in a conversation, it is, again, important to "check signals." If you sense that what a person is saying is contradictory to their body language, ask them to clarify what they mean. Both parties need to recognize that it is important to validate any messages that may not be clear.

Discussing the value of signal checking as a part of your communication guidelines can be helpful. It may be important for teachers and administrators to spend some time reviewing the facial expressions and body language associated with particular emotions to ensure they are accurate in their communication, and to help them interpret the messages that others may be sending.

A chart of human emotions developed by Jourmana Medlej can be found at: http://majnouna.com/creation/emotut.jpg.

While this chart does not reflect all cultural variances of facial expressions and body language, it is a starting place for reviewing and discussing what we "see" when we look at people while they are supposedly displaying an emotion. Using this chart, or asking individuals to mimic the facial expressions and body language reflective of particular emotions can be an interesting activity for a faculty meeting. This can be an informative discussion, as accurately reading students' emotions, as well as colleagues, can help facilitate positive interactions throughout the school.

Tone of voice is another key component of nonverbal language. The use of inflection, or paralanguage, as it is called, is often what is remembered more than the words a speaker uses. Paralanguage is the meaning that occurs in conversations beyond, or in addition to, the words we speak. The match or mismatch between what is said and the tone used is very important. If the tone of voice matches the words, the message is believable. If the tone is incongruent with the words, then the tone, not the words, conveys the message.

Matching tone to the verbal message is very important in any interpersonal communication. If a principal tells a teacher that she wants to support him but says this using a contradictory or inconsistent tone, it is the tone, not the words, that will be heard. If a principal tells a teacher, following an observation, that he or she likes the way the teacher called on her students in class, but says it hesitantly while looking away, this is a mismatch between the words and the paralanguage.

In this situation described above, the principal is sending a nonverbal cue that he or she does not necessarily mean what the spoken words convey. Awareness of our own use of paralanguage is an important factor in creating messages that can be heard accurately by the receiver of the message. Identifying paralanguage as a component of communication is important for any discussion regarding observation and evaluation processes.

Administrators may want to try the following exercises to heighten their awareness of nonverbal communication and the use of paralanguage.

Nonverbal Practice 1

Say the following phrases to a peer or videotape yourself. Try to convey the positive emotion listed in the parentheses. If you are using a videotape, watch your physical stances, gestures, and facial expressions and listen to your verbal tone when you play back the video.

If you are having another educator watch you, have your partner write down and tell you what they see in your face and body and what tone they hear. Answer the questions at the end of the exercise. The goal is to get a sense of how accurately you are able to convey these emotions.

"I think you're doing a great job!" (enthusiasm)

"When you said that to the students, what was their response?" (wondering)

"The class was on task, even if they were a bit loud." (confidence)

"It's hard to find time to create your lesson plans." (supportive)

"Do you want me to give you some suggestions?" (questioning)

"I really enjoyed watching the students interact in their small groups yesterday." (pleased)

"It's tough when a parent gets upset with you." (empathy)

"I saw what you did with the fourth grade math lesson on fractions yesterday." (approval)

"Tell me how you manage and support your students with learning needs." (encouraging)

"I hear your concerns; let's talk about how we can address them." (positive/helpful)

"This issue will take some further conversation." (firm)

"Tell me about your students." (interested)

Follow-up questions:

- From your observations or the feedback you received, describe how your nonverbal signals matched your messages.
- What might you need to do to change your tone, facial expressions, or body language to more accurately reflect the words you are speaking?

Principals who discussed the questions following their practice with the dialogue exercises above noted that it was not always easy to match their vocal tone and nonverbal signals. Yet, developing an awareness of the use of inflection and the ways in which they were able to create the tone they were trying to convey was important. By listening to themselves and working with peers, the administrators felt they were able to monitor their own use of tone and nonverbal signals to create accurate messages.

There was agreement among the participating administrators about the importance of conveying an accurate message to teachers, especially following an observation. They discussed the fact that if teachers are told that they are improving, but also hear the words verbalized in a tone that reflects uncertainly, they probably will not believe what is said. This leads to distrust and a lack of self-confidence on the part of the listener or unwillingness to accept what was said.

If administrators have set up expectations that they are going to generate honest communication, then teachers expect honesty. If they get a sense that their principal does not mean what they say, the relationship is damaged and the potential for effective learning is diminished.

Administrators can use the following dialogue exercises to identify nonverbal and paralinguistic signals that accompany negative emotions. By becoming aware of these signals, principals can work to avoid using them unintentionally.

Nonverbal Practice 2

Practice saying the phrases listed below using the identified negative emotion and accompanying nonverbal signals. Videotape yourself or have another principal provide feedback. While the emotion attached to the message may seem unrealistic, this exercise strengthens your awareness and control of the tone, stance, gestures, and facial expressions that accompany *negative* emotions, so you can monitor your own interactions.

"I think you're doing a great job." (hesitancy)

"When you said that to the students, what was their response?" (irritation)

"The class was on task, even if they were loud." (concern)

"It's hard to find time to create your lesson plans." (disbelief)

"Do you want me to give you some suggestions?" (demanding)

"I enjoyed watching the students interact in their small groups yesterday." (distracted)

"It's tough when a parent gets upset with you." (sarcasm)

"I saw what you did with the fourth grade math lesson on fractions yesterday." (worry)

"Tell me how you manage and support your students with learning needs." (forceful)

"I hear your concerns; let's talk about how we can address them." (irritated)

"This issue will take some further conversation." (angry)

"Tell me about your students." (unconcerned)

Follow-up questions:

- As you listened, what did you pay more attention to, the words or the emotion (nonverbal message) of each phrase?
- How would you feel if you heard these messages with that prescribed tone?
- What could you do to create a more positive tone/emotion to match these verbal and nonverbal messages?

These questions bring up the contradictions that occur when a person says something that might seem positive but utters it with a negative tone and/or uses negative body language. When such a contradiction occurs, the listener focuses on the emotion conveyed, not the words.

It is important that principals practice matching their tone to the words they speak, especially when conversing with a teacher in relation to evaluation or improvement issues. Awareness of tone, facial expression, and body language help individuals match verbal and nonverbal messages. Administrators can use a mirror or video cameras or practice with a friend to increase their ability to monitor their tone and nonverbal messages.

The following aspects of nonverbal communication, which may be culture or gender based, should also be given focused attention in all communication processes. These communicative components can influence the interpretation of conversation and, in turn, impact relationships that are needed to facilitate ongoing learning. It is important that administrators explore these aspects of communication with their teachers as well.

Proximity: Everyone has a comfort level regarding the personal space that surrounds them during conversations, so standing too close to a person you are talking to can be disquieting. A teacher usually perceives the principal as having more power (e.g., they are the "boss" of the school), so when the administrator stands quite close during a discussion, it may heighten the sense of dominance.

Misuse of proximity is not productive when trying to develop trust. If principals feel crowded or find they are leaning slightly away during conversations, they may want to identify this issue and discuss views of "personal space" with the individual. If teachers or principals feel that the other person exhibits proximity-violating behaviors, it will be important for them to acknowledge this fact.

Both parties need to check signals to ensure that they are aware of and responding to these issues appropriately. Naming the concern and sharing perspectives about proximity in conversations is an important step in creating positive communication patterns.

Turn taking: A speaker who does not allow someone to complete what they are saying, but who jumps in with comments or suggestions, can give the impression of not caring about the other person's comments. Interrupting minimizes the other speaker's contributions to the conversation. In open communication, each member of the conversation has an equal right to speak, and taking turns is important. Interrupting and cutting off conversation can inhibit the careful listening that is a part of effective communication.

Conversations between principals and teachers should not center on one person doing all the talking. The discussion should be about what happened in the classroom—given from both perspectives. Both individuals should be sharing ideas, experiences, and information to reach conclusions about educational practice. This means that both individuals should participate equally in the dialogue. Identifying differences in turn-taking behavior and working to listen carefully can minimize incorrect perceptions and foster positive, effective discussions.

It is important for both the teacher and principal to identify their tendencies regarding turn taking. Some people wait for a more overt acknowledgment identifying that it is their turn to speak. However, American culture often uses very slight pauses where the other speaker is supposed to jump in with their comments. If the listener does not pick up on pauses as a cue to add their thoughts, it can feel to the speaker as though they have been given permission to just keep talking.

Providing a pause and waiting for the other person to add their thoughts is important. If pausing does not produce input from a speaker, it is helpful to ask questions that invite their response. Because the principal is often seen as the "lead" in conversation (particularly a discussion related to evaluation), it is important for the administrator to note the turn-taking processes and support and encourage opportunities for both individuals to share their thoughts.

Eye contact: There is an expectation in North American and European cultures that individuals look each other in the eye when they converse. If the listener looks away, the speaker may perceive a lack of interest or view the individual who looks away as dishonest or shifty. On the other hand, when someone stares during a conversation, it can be disconcerting.

Principals should strive to use the appropriate level of eye contact to reflect their interest and support. Checking signals regarding the use of eye contact is important, especially if one observes behaviors that differ from their own. Administrators should strive to identify and provide a comfortable visual connection during conversations.

Listening: There is a typical listening stance used in the United States that identifies that someone is paying attention to what is being said in a conversation. Leaning forward slightly and focusing eye contact on the speaker, signals that the listener is being attentive. Eye contact, nodding, smiling, and other facial expressions also identify that the listener is focused on what is being said and is "tracking" with the speaker. Effective listening also means asking occasional questions to ensure that the listener is on the same page as the speaker.

Principals who are good listeners ensure there is balance in a conversation and give their teachers plenty of opportunity to talk. Listening does not mean offering answers or solutions but is simply about absorbing and reflecting on what the other person is saying. Listening can be a powerful support for open communication, if the listener is truly concentrating and focused on the speaker's message. Principals need to be sure they work to concentrate on the message being sent, not on figuring out a response.

Being "in the moment" is an expression that reflects this idea of good listening, where the listener is trying to eliminate mental noise and focus on the message being conveyed by the other individual. Principals need to practice being "in the moment" when communicating with faculty.

Use of time: Allowing significant time for a conversation to occur is another signal that a message is important. If principals set up a time to talk and then change the scheduled time or look at their watches and seem eager to get going during the meeting, teachers will feel that what they have to say is not important—or that they themselves are not valued.

Failure to use time well undermines trust and inhibits open communication. Some individuals and cultures are not as time sensitive as others, and administrators and teachers need to address these differences if they occur. Discussions about the use of time and what it means to each individual to "be on time" can help foster understanding and develop a positive communication process.

Age and experience can also impact the communication process. An experienced teacher will appreciate honest and open communication, particularly if the principal acknowledges and shows respect for the wisdom gathered over years. Principals need to check their communication processes and language choices to clearly communicate respect when working with a veteran educator. They need to show value for the years of experience mature teachers bring to discussions.

Peer observations by other experienced members of the faculty should be encouraged between veteran educators. Offering peer interactions as an additional part of the evaluative process can be a key component in effectively working with veteran teachers. When two colleagues work together and give equal respect to each other's expertise and experience, the potential for mutual growth is increased.

Using peer observation processes communicates respect for the expertise held by experienced faculty members.

Peer interactions may also be more effective and generate less resistance than traditional principal interactions when teachers work with experienced faculty members. It can also be helpful if principals make connections between new methodologies, expectations, and the practices veteran teachers are currently using in order to validate the teacher's work. Many teachers can adapt innovations and hone their skills when they see the connection or relationship between the practices they have been using and the new concepts expected of them.

The process of good communication requires both parties in a conversation set goals for the discussion. These goals may be based on an upcoming evaluation process to familiarize individuals with the evaluation tool. It may be that the goal is in response to data gathered from a previous evaluation or observation. This cyclic process involves both the principal and the teacher and sets up a process for them to work together to enhance student growth.

It takes time to change gears and do something differently, and principals need to allow time for all teachers to gradually develop their comfort level and expertise with any new concept. The various steps in the cyclic evaluative dialogue process included below will help guide this developmental process.

By paying attention to the process of communication, principals can develop trust and provide for open communication. Even when they are of varying gender, race, age, or experience, communication can be effective when participants in the relationship acknowledge and address communication components and styles. In doing so, they will generate greater levels of trust.

Teachers will not share important issues or concerns if they are unsure of their principal's response, so little will be accomplished despite the use of an effective evaluation tool. In order to have important discussions that lead to improved teaching and higher levels of learning for students, principals must continually use mentoring skills and check signals to foster trust and open communication.

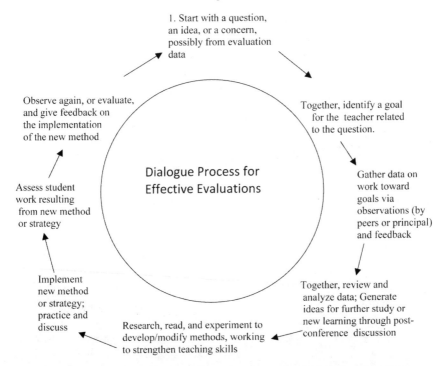

Figure 3.1. Evaluation Dialogue Process This is a model for evaluative dialogue process and provides a process for conversation between administrators and faculty.

NOTES

1. Pauker, R. and Hibbard, M. (2013). *Matching Your Message to the Audience. A Practical Guide to Structuring Language for New Administrators.* Lanham, MD: Rowman & Littlefield.

2. Manusov, V. (2009). Negative affect reciprocity. In H. T. Reis and S. K. Sprecher (Eds.), Encyclopedia of Human Relationships. Thousand Oaks, CA: Sage.

Chapter Four

Aligning Dialogue to the Evaluation Tool

A review of current evaluation tools to provide insight into the knowledge base and skill sets required of educators today is the focus of this chapter. It identifies how principals can use an evaluation tool as a basis for teacher development. The main concepts from the Marzano and Danielson evaluation models are presented and ideas for review and community development around the expectations in each of these tools are provided.

In order to provide teachers a view of their teaching and learning practices, principals visit and observe classrooms. The principal's goal for a classroom observation should be to serve as a mirror, reflecting for the teacher what was observed and using this information for further conversation and ongoing learning. The observation/evaluation process gives teachers another perspective to help them see their work and examine student learning to identify areas for further development.

Depending on their own styles and interests, some principals may focus on certain areas of a teacher's practices more than others. Because of this natural focusing tendency, it is important that both administrators and teachers know up front what *lens*—the description of professional practice that is used as a guide for evaluation—a principal is using to view the classroom. Without a defined focal point, the principal may overlook some of what is happening in the teacher's instructional practices by giving too much credence to a particular event.

The use of an evaluation tool for formative assessment is critical in mentoring and supporting teachers. Research identifies the importance of having teaching and learning standards that link with the daily work of teachers as a focus for observations and evaluations.[1] Using an evaluation tool with standards and criteria as a lens provides a model and language to help support ongoing teacher development.

It is very important to review this lens prior to a summative evaluation. Teachers need to have time to learn and use the criteria identified in a lens prior to a formal evaluation. Principals working to support teachers will want to use the tool to shape learning and provide formative evaluations that are documented only for the teacher. These formative assessments are used to help teachers see what they do well and what they need to work on prior to being involved in a formal, summative evaluation that "counts."

Many school districts have already developed summative teacher evaluation tools to be used with all K–12 faculty. Previously, most evaluations were given only to beginning teachers, based on the thinking that once a teacher was awarded tenure, there was little need (or time) for formal evaluations. These newly updated evaluation tools and processes, based on teacher observations, are aligned to the specific practices that have been identified as necessary to enhance learning for all students.

An evaluation tool acts as a lens for viewing professional practice, and there are several evaluation models available. What is most important is that there *is* an evaluation tool, or lens, and that the language used in the tool is clearly understood by all faculty members and administrators. Without a lens to provide a shared understanding of what constitutes effective teaching, an evelution process may be unfocused and unproductive. Principals working to create positive relationships with teachers need to ensure that faculty are well versed in the language and expectations of the lens.

The various instruments available for use as a lens have similar components. Principals need to be familiar with these components and consider how they describe a teacher's efforts and skills. Rather than gathering evidence of classroom interactions randomly, administrators need to use an evaluation instrument as a lens to focus their selection of evidence and to help teachers identify areas of strength as well as areas for growth.

Together, principals and teachers need to identify which components of the evaluation tool will be the focus of any particular classroom visit and create a plan for each observation session. While a summative evaluation may address all components of a lens, formative evaluations should narrow the focus so that teachers can identify their strengths and work on enhancing their weaker areas. Starting with the teacher's strengths and giving a choice as to which criteria will be the focus of early observations will help teachers maintain trust in the process.

Whichever tool a district is using for evaluation, it is imperative that principals incorporate the language and emphasis of that evaluation tool in their conversations and interactions with teachers. Administrators and teachers must develop a common understanding of the lens used to observe and evaluate. The evaluation tool, or lens, needs to be used to provide pre-observation training. In addition, the criteria language must be incorporated throughout faculty development as well as throughout all observation and evaluation processes.

If this evaluation process and lens is new to teachers in a district, the principal needs to provide opportunities for discussing the language and providing examples of teaching that exemplify the expected practices. Principals can do this by providing teachers with opportunities to observe educators who effectively integrate the knowledge and skills indicated in the model. Following up the demonstrations with open discussions about the strategies used in the model lesson will help clarify expectations.

Such processes enable faculty to see the teaching criteria in action, hear various perspectives, and consider ways to incorporate the skill into their own teaching. Principals should also provide opportunities for faculty to visit other schools, attend workshop sessions focused on the methodology, and view videos of effective teaching. All of these learning events and discussions are important prerequisites to the use of an evaluation tool.

Teachers need to understand the organizational structure, expectations, and criteria that will be used to view their work. They must clearly understand what is expected of them, and this will require faculty training and discussion regarding the lens prior to its use. Principals who embrace their role as mentor must make a commitment to provide resources—both materials and time—that will enable teachers to develop or hone the skills being addressed in the evaluation.

A principal who wants to mentor his faculty may create a schedule that provides early-release time to generate additional faculty meetings for learning. With supports in place, teachers can strengthen the identified best practices and enhance their skills while preparing for the evaluation. All of this will benefit the children in their classrooms.

In some situations, a teacher might still be resistant to a principal's comments or suggestions, even after efforts have been made to develop a positive relationship and learn about the tool. Having a well-defined lens gives credence to any recommendations for growth because the evaluation tool provides specific, researched criteria related to effective teaching. The criteria are not just something the administrators want to see happen; their comments are based on expectations that are generated by experts.

A lens allows administrators to observe from a balanced perspective using pre-defined criteria and language that has been shared and reviewed with faculty. If a faculty member's teaching style is unique or different from the principal's style, the lens provides a common reference point and keeps the observations and comments "on target."

Although principals have traditionally evaluated teaching through the use of classroom observations, where the teacher's work is most apparent, lesson and unit planning are also a critical element of effective teaching and learning. Positive, supportive interactions in the classroom do not occur random-ly—teachers must thoughtfully consider how to create a climate conducive to learning and develop plans to make this happen.

The work a teacher does beyond the classroom has a huge impact on his or her effectiveness: connecting with parents, working with colleagues, and continuing their own learning—all are important aspects of supporting stu-dent learning. Principals will want to look at their teachers' planning prac-tices and professional interactions as well as what happens in the classroom to get a full picture of the teacher's work. This will necessitate conversations beyond the classroom observations in order to discuss all teaching and learn-ing events that the teacher is involved in regarding their students.

Currently, there are two nationally known evaluation instruments used primarily by principals in U.S. school districts. These tools ask for evidence of a teacher's work in four broad areas: planning, instruction, classroom interactions, and professionalism. Both of these lenses describe what teachers should know and be able to do, using criteria that identify the various levels of knowledge and skill regarding the teacher's work.

Training and assessment offered by the authors of these national tools are designed to create consistency so that principals can clearly see evidence of teachers' work in the domains being presented in these lenses. All domains are considered equally important for effective teaching, and the criteria with-in each domain are measured against rubrics developed by the authors. Ad-ministrators who use one of these lenses should engage in training experi-ences to help them clearly view the classroom through the tool's particular focus.

A district needs to provide learning opportunities, either through national training sessions or through locally developed "train the trainer" models for principals. This learning can occur *with* the faculty so that there is shared learning taking place. Without such training, there is little hope that an evalu-ation process will be implemented effectively, or that teachers will benefit and learn from the evaluation. Principals need to be knowledgeable and comfortable with the lens used for evaluation.

The Framework for Teaching Evaluation Instrument and *Scales and Evi-dence for the Marzano Teacher Evaluation Model* are two of the nationally developed evaluation tools that identify the key components of good teach-ing. When observed in the classroom, these various principles, domains, components, or dimensions all indicate effective practices. Principals must keep in mind that although it is easy to use these criteria solely to determine what teachers cannot do, they should also be used to identify what teachers do well.

The data gathered from use of one of these tools also provides insights into areas where teachers can direct their learning. Without a lens to focus a classroom observation, principals and teachers can overlook areas of strength or miss areas where further learning is needed.

Textbox 4.1 shows the list of criteria described in *The Framework for Teaching,* an evaluation tool developed by Charlotte Danielson:

Domain 1: Planning and Preparation

Component 1a: Demonstrating Knowledge of Content and Pedagogy
Knowledge of content and the structure of the discipline
Knowledge of prerequisite relationships
Knowledge of content-related pedagogy

Component 1b: Demonstrating Knowledge of Students
Knowledge of child and adolescent development
Knowledge of the learning process
Knowledge of students' skills, knowledge, and language proficien-cy
Knowledge of students' interests and cultural heritage
Knowledge of students' special needs

Component 1c: Selecting Instructional Outcomes
Value, sequence, and alignment
Clarity
Balance
Suitability for diverse students

Component 1d: Demonstrating Knowledge of Resources
Resources for classroom use
Resources to extend content knowledge and pedagogy
Resources for students

Component 1e: Designing Coherent Instruction
Learning activities
Instructional materials and resources
Instructional groups
Lesson and unit structure

Component 1f: Designing Student Assessments
Congruence with instructional outcomes
Criteria and standards
Design of formative assessments

Use for planning

Domain 2: The Classroom Environment

Component 2a: Creating an Environment of Respect and Rapport
    Teacher interaction with students, including both words and actions
    Student interactions with other students, including both words and
actions

Component 2b: Establishing a Culture for Learning
    Importance of the content and of learning
    Expectations for learning and achievement
    Student pride in work

Component 2c: Managing Classroom Procedures
    Management of instructional groups
    Management of transitions
    Management of materials and supplies
    Performance of classroom routines

Component 2d: Managing Student Behavior
    Expectations
    Monitoring of student behavior
    Response to student misbehavior

Component 2e: Organizing Physical Space
    Safety and accessibility
    Arrangement of furniture and use of physical resources

Domain 3: Instruction

Component 3a: Communicating Clearly and Accurately with Students
    Expectations for learning
    Directions for activities
    Explanations of content
    Use of oral and written language

Component 3b: Using Questioning and Discussion Techniques
    Quality of questions/prompts
    Discussion techniques
    Student participation

Component 3c: Engaging Students in Learning
    Activities and assignments
    Grouping of students
    Instructional materials and resources
    Structure and pacing

Component 3d: Using Assessment in Instruction
    Assessment criteria
    Monitoring of student learning
    Feedback to students
    Student self-assessment and monitoring of progress

Component 3e: Demonstrating Flexibility and Responsiveness
    Lesson adjustment
    Response to students
    Persistence

Domain 4: Professional Responsibilities

Component 4a: Reflecting on Teaching
    Accuracy
    Use in future teaching

Component 4b: Maintaining Accurate Records
    Student completion of assignments
    Student progress in learning
    Non-instructional records

Component 4c: Communicating with Families
    Information about the instructional program
    Information about individual students
    Engagement of families in the instructional program

Component 4d: Participating in the Professional Community
    Relationships with colleagues
    Involvement in a culture of professional inquiry
    Service to the school
    Participation in school and district projects

Component 4e: Growing and Developing Professionally
    Enhancement of content knowledge and pedagogical skill

Receptivity to feedback from colleagues
Service to the profession

Component 4f: Showing Professionalism
Integrity and ethical conduct
Service to students
Advocacy
Decision making
Compliance with school and district regulations

Dr. Robert Marzano has also generated an observation tool that includes a detailed model for organizing teaching and learning that contains numerous specific criteria. All criteria in Marzano's evaluation tool fall under four domains:

1. Classroom Strategies and Behaviors;
2. Planning and Preparing;
3. Reflecting on Teaching;
4. Collegiality and Professionalism.

The Marzano Teacher Evaluation Model, prepared by Marzano Research Laboratory,[2] contain sixty specific criteria for teachers and observers to consider when reviewing teaching and learning in a classroom, along with rubrics and examples for each criteria. Danielson's *The Framework for Teaching*[3] also incorporates rubrics and examples, but the main difference between *The Marzano Teacher Evaluation Model* and Danielson's *The Framework for Teaching* is the number of criteria to be considered.

The Marzano scales also frame the evaluation tool with questions to consider when designing learning events. Marzano has identified nine of these "design questions" to consider while preparing or evaluating a teaching event. These design questions, which are incorporated into the first and second domains, are as follows:

• What will I do to establish and communicate learning goals, track student progress, and celebrate success?
• What will I do to help students effectively interact with new knowledge?
• What will I do to help students practice and deepen their understanding of new knowledge?
• What will I do to help students generate and test hypotheses about new knowledge?
• What will I do to engage students?

- What will I do to recognize and acknowledge adherence or lack of adherence to rules and procedures?
- What will I do to establish and maintain effective relationships with students?
- What will I do to communicate high expectations for all students?
- What will I do to develop effective lessons, organized into an effective unit?

Within each question are subcomponents. There are fifteen of these elements under design question number 5 alone; giving Marzano's scale a length and level of detail that reflects the complexities of teaching. Specifically, Domain 1 is based on Marzano's earlier work[4] and contains forty-one elements (or instructional categories) that are organized under the design questions. The final design question, Developing Effective Lessons Organized into a Cohesive Unit, is contained in Domain 2: Planning and Preparing. The third and fourth domains do not contain design questions.

Marzano's full scale of sixty elements (with rubrics and examples) defines effective teaching and learning. This level of specificity provides principals and teachers with a comprehensive list of components that can be considered as a guide to support teacher learning as well as a lens for teacher evaluation.

Because Marzano's scales provide such extensive guidelines for evaluation, principals must consider which elements will be addressed initially or whether fewer criteria, such as those presented by Danielson's model, would be most effective for their faculty.

Deciding which lens to use, done in partnership with faculty to create buy-in and shared understanding, is an important communicative process that is vital for the effective use of the evaluation tool. Faculty members need to be a part of the decision-making process in identifying which evaluation tool will be adopted by the school or district.

Whichever assessment tool is adopted for use by a school or district, all the elements used to evaluate teachers must be studied by the faculty. Without developing an understanding of the language for each criteria or examining examples, teachers may find it challenging to address the components effectively. A lack of understanding of the tool will also be challenging for administrators trying to support their faculty and evaluate fairly. Studying the tool, breaking it down, and focusing on a few elements at a time will be a productive process and will enable all to develop an understanding of the expectations. The elements of Marzano's *Teacher Evaluation Model* are found in figure 4.1.

When administrators and faculty are in the process of selecting the lens that will be used during observations to evaluate faculty, comparing the models can help with the decision. The two evaluation tools identified in this

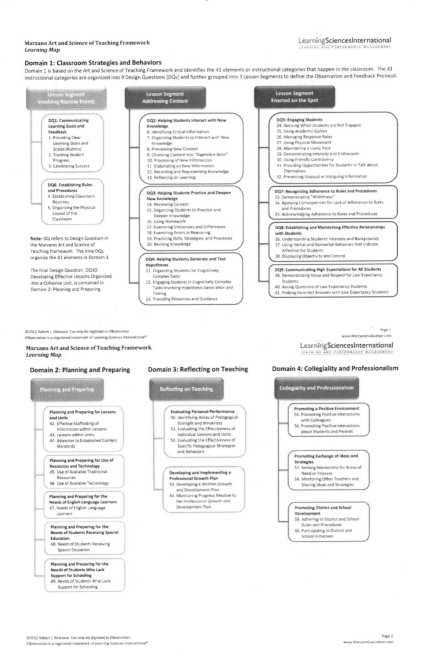

Figure 4.1. **Marzano Teacher Evaluation Model Learning Map Used with permission.** *Marzano Center Teacher Observation Protocol for the 2014 Marzano Teacher Evaluation Model* by Dr. Robert J. Marzano. Copyright 2013 by Learning Sciences International. All rights reserved.

text should be analyzed to determine the best fit for viewing and supporting teaching in their school. Any nationally or locally designed evaluation tool being considered should also be compared to the two mentioned here. If teachers participate in this decision, the use of the selected tool will be a more collaborative process.

To provide a means for this review, consider the two evaluation tools identified in this text and note your answers to the following questions as well as the reason(s) behind your answer:

1. What is similar in these models? What is different or unique in each model?
2. Which model do you find most compatible with the language you typically use to talk about teaching?
3. Which lens would you feel most comfortable using as a tool for supporting ongoing learning?
4. Which lens would you want to use for formative assessments?
5. Which would you choose to use as a summative evaluation tool?
6. Should the tool be the same in all circumstances—for formative and summative assessments as well as to support ongoing learning?
7. Depending on the developmental level of a teacher and/or years of experience, which model would you utilize?

Share your perspective with a colleague. Do you agree or disagree about the purpose behind the use of these observation tools in your school or district?

If you have yet to determine the lens your school or district will implement, complete the chart in table 4.1 to help you make your decision. This will enable principals and teachers to reflect on their perspectives regarding the various observation tools and come to a consensus regarding which evaluation tool will be implemented.

Evaluation Tool:	The Framework for Teaching (Danielson)	Teacher Evaluation Scales (Marzano)	Other national tool?	Locally developed lens?
What are the unique components of the model?				
Is the language used familiar to faculty and administrators? (examples)				

Can tool be used for novice and experienced teachers? (why or why not?)
Ease/cost of implementation?
Faculty development needs prior to implementation?
Administrator development needs prior to implementation?

Principals need to develop a clear understanding of what is meant by each component of the evaluation tool and help their teachers acquire this knowledge as well. What does a particular component look like in action? What does it sound like in the classroom? What will students and/or teachers be doing that reflects the language of the lens? Using a lens as a discussion tool prior to evaluation enables everyone involved to develop a common understanding of the educative processes and practices being reviewed.

The evaluation tool should also be a focal point for identifying ongoing learning and support for teachers. Developing a clear understanding of the expectations inherent in the evaluation tool is a key element in the mentoring interaction between teachers and the principal. There must be a common understanding of the evaluation tool or any data generated by the evaluation will be inaccurate. It is not a fair evaluation if those being reviewed do not clearly understand the language of the tool.

Principals need to take the time to familiarize themselves with the language of the evaluation tool selected by their district and ensure teachers are also aware of the specifics within each tool. What is expected for each particular criterion? What will the teacher and/or the students be doing? What should occur in the planning to ensure that a particular criterion is met? Unless this process of "unpacking" the components of the lens occurs, the benefits for teacher support and evaluation are limited because the tool is measuring something that has not been clearly communicated to teachers.

This does not mean that teachers do not have the knowledge and skills inherent in an evaluation tool, but it might be that the work of preparing for daily classes has created an internalization of classroom practices. Teachers need to have opportunities to explicitly discuss the language of the lens so they are comfortable with the evaluation and understand the need to articulate the specifics involved in their work.

For formative evaluations to be successful learning and mentoring experiences, and for summative evaluations to be fair and accurate, ongoing use and study of the language from a specific lens is important. Principals can make their classroom observations highly insightful for their teachers by developing a deep understanding of the lens.

Taking time to practice applying the lens, using guiding questions, and reflecting on what is observed in the classroom will help principals prepare to work successfully with their teachers. As with any skill, administrators must spend time familiarizing themselves with the process of using the tool in order to mentor faculty successfully and "see" the interactions in a classroom through the language of the lens.

NOTES

1. Darling-Hammond, L. (2013) *Getting Teacher Evaluation Right: What Really Matters for Effectiveness and Improvement,* New York: Teachers College Press.
2. Marzano, R. (2013). *Scales and Evidence for the Marzano Teacher Evaluation Model.* Learning Sciences. www.marzanocenter.com.
3. Danielson, C. (2011). *The Framework for Teaching Evaluation Instrument.* Princeton, NJ; The Danielson Group. www.danielsongroup.org.
4. Marzano, R. (2007). *The Art and Science of Teaching.* Reston, VA: ASCD.

Chapter Five

Questions to Support Teacher Learning

Ideas for enhancing the questioning process to help teachers hear and utilize feedback from evaluations are the focus of this chapter. A chart and practice scenarios are offered to enable administrators to consider crafting effective questions to facilitate teacher learning.

Imagine that a principal walks into a classroom and takes a random photograph that includes all of the students and the teacher. What might this snapshot tell the administrator about the teaching and learning going on in that room? The photo might show two students facing each other, seemingly engaged in conversation, while the rest of the students are facing the teacher and holding their pencils to their notebooks.

Would it be correct for the observer to assume that the two students facing each other are off task and chatting about something other than the lesson? Should the principal assume that all the students looking at the teacher are engaged in the lesson? Not knowing what is being said, the observer cannot be sure. A principal has to hear the conversation and observe the context to reflect on the teaching and has to talk to those involved to know what they are thinking.

Gathering data about what goes on in a classroom means going beyond taking a quick snapshot. Walk-throughs are often used by principals, but they do not show the entire picture, nor do they provide time to discuss the teaching events observed in this quick review. A critical element of the evaluation process is a conversation about the observation. It is necessary to ask questions and discuss all data gathered in an observation, using appropriate communication skills, to ensure that the context of the lesson's events is clear.

Effective teaching evaluations need to include a conversation before and after the observation in the classroom. The components of the evaluation tool that will be addressed in the observation should be identified during a pre-observation conference, with the specific criteria and data that will be gathered clearly defined. These specifications become the focus of the observation and the post-observation conference as well, and are the basis for feedback to the teacher.

The administrator and the teacher first need to talk about what will occur in a lesson and what the principal will be looking for during an observation. The lesson is then taught, followed by a discussion about the lesson. In the post-conversation, the teacher should identify the strengths of the teaching episode, with additional comments about what might have influenced classroom events to provide context for the lesson. The principal needs to consider if what was expected to occur in the lesson did indeed happen. This includes discussing how the teacher's planning impacted the resulting lesson.

As they confer about a lesson, administrators need to use the predetermined lens to focus their conversation and provide feedback. In a formative evaluation, it is vital to determine ahead of time if all criteria, or only a few specific expectations, will be the focus. The formative evaluation is like a practice run—giving the principal and the teacher the opportunity to utilize their knowledge and skills related to the lens without the resulting data being used as a definitive statement of the teaching event.

The lesson debriefing needs to describe the data gathered during the observation. There are data-gathering techniques and tools that can be used to help administrators describe what they saw and heard during the observation, related to the criteria. Effective questioning processes can also provide a means for administrators to ensure that teachers have the opportunity to clarify and articulate their perspective of the lesson and how, or if, criteria were met.

Without evidence, a post-observation conversation can become centered on what administrators thought they observed rather than what actually occurred, and opinions and judgments can be formed that might not be accurate. Identifying the criteria and the data-gathering process prior to the observation ensures that both the teacher and the principal are on the same page regarding the evidence that will be gathered. The more specific the criteria language, the easier it is to ascertain whether the criteria were met.

As mentioned earlier in this text, the need for specific and effective language is crucial in all steps of the observation. An administrator who is trying to support faculty members must be clear, concise, and honest when naming the criteria to be observed and when speaking about the evidence gathered in the lesson. Principals need to clearly communicate what they observed so teachers can reflect and respond, using similar terms. Using specific language to share both the intended criteria and the observed data will provide clarity for all involved in the observation and evaluation process.

Data provides a mirror to help teachers view their practice clearly. Research states that "feedback refers to the process of securing information enabling change through adjustment or calibration of efforts in order to bring a person closer to a well-defined goal."[1] Teachers need to see the data and hear the evidence gathered during the observation—and reflect about what occurred. It is through this feedback/reflection process that teacher growth will occur.

A benefit of considering the implications of data gathered during an observation is that teachers enhance their own problem-solving skills as they analyze the information. In addition, the data provides specific language for principals as they offer suggestions and guidance to their teachers. By adhering to the language of the criteria, administrators can use the evaluation tool, or lens, to enhance teacher knowledge and skills.

In an initial formative observation, the principal and teacher should identify one or two components from the lens they are using as a focus so the teacher is not overwhelmed. In later observations, administrators can work toward gathering evidence for all components of the selected model. The choice of a lens provides a clear focus for the pre-observation conversation: teachers are made aware of the specifics they need to identify in planning their classroom practice, and principals know that they may need to ask guiding questions related to that specific area.

When teachers and principals meet to talk about an upcoming observation, the teacher needs to identify the objectives for the lesson and articulate his or her reasons for choosing these goals. Educators should also describe the steps they will follow or the structure they will use to engage students in the learning and to meet all students' learning needs. They need to identify how they plan to determine whether the students are successful in meeting objectives—what assessment will be used.

During this discussion, both parties should be aware of the lens that is being used. For example, if Danielson's *Framework for Teaching* is used, teachers will know that Component 1a requires them to demonstrate their knowledge of content and pedagogy. The pre-conference provides a time for teachers to articulate what they know about content and pedagogy related to the lesson and their students, as they describe their plans for the upcoming learning event, using the language of the lens.

The pre-observation conference is also a time for principals to clarify anything the teacher says that does not provide sufficient detail. Probing with guiding questions to hear more about a particular aspect of the lesson is an important dimension of the administrator's role. This conversation should provide the principal with deeper understanding of the teacher's planning skills. By asking guiding questions, the principal ensures that the teacher remembers to describe all components of the lesson, her knowledge of her students, and anything else that supports her rationale for the lesson.

The give-and-take of this interaction allows teachers to expand their thinking and articulate the choices they have made when planning the lesson. When teachers clarify the reasons for their plans and address the lesson details in response to questions, they help ensure that the observer has a clear picture of their planning process.

The pre-observation conference is a critical component of any evaluation. Sometimes a lesson plan might not be clear. The conference might lead to the creation of a refined lesson plan, or it might indicate to the principal that the teacher needs some additional resources in order to put together a lesson plan that meets the lens's expectations. Observing a lesson without prior conversation can lead to misconceptions about the teacher's plans.

For example, an administrator might want to focus on management issues during a lesson, but the teacher is working to implement active learning and knows there will be some challenges. In this case, the observer might fail to completely understand what occurred in the classroom, because his or her focus was only on management. Teachers should clarify if there is something specific they want the principal to focus on during the observation or explain if there is an underlying reason for their choices that might not be apparent to an uninformed observer.

These pre-observation conferences do not always need to be face-to-face interactions, but it is more helpful for both parties to clearly "hear" the nonverbal aspect of the conversation by being present in person. The pre-observation can be in written form, with teachers sharing lesson plans and offering written notes to explain the rationale for the method and content selection. An e-mail exchange of plans and feedback can provide a convenient way for teachers and principals to review what is going to happen in an observation.

Electronic or written messages alone, however, may not provide for a clear exchange of ideas and information, even though using e-mail can help both individuals manage their time more effectively. If scheduling conflicts prevent a meeting prior to the lesson, a phone conversation is another option. At the very least, a brief conversation right before the lesson, based on written comments and plans previously shared, can help prevent misunderstandings and ensure that both individuals are on the same page at the start of the lesson.

The questions below are examples that could be asked in a pre-observation conference to gather information about an upcoming observation and a teacher's planning process. The rationale behind asking these particular questions is also stated. It is important to note that the language or focus for each observation may vary according to the lens/evaluation tool being used, so these questions may need to be adapted.

PRE-CONFERENCE QUESTIONS

Review the sample questions listed below and discuss them with another principal, or reflect on how they might impact a pre-observation conference. Decide if the language "fits" your style. Then generate additional or alternative questions you would like to use in a pre-observation conference.

1. What is it you want your students to know and/or be able to do at the end of this lesson? (objective/knowledge of content/overall assessment)
2. Why did you choose this particular focus for your lesson? (purpose/rationale)
3. How do you think your students will do with this lesson? (knowledge of students)
4. How will you address the various needs of your learners during this lesson? (knowledge of differentiation and knowledge of diverse learning needs)
5. How will you create connections between this lesson, yesterday's lesson, and tomorrow's lesson? (use of prior knowledge and sequence of a learning event)
6. How are you planning to carry out_____? [specify the instructional strategy/learning activity]. (knowledge of instructional practices; sequence; need for directions; pedagogy)
7. How will you know that the students have met the objective? (assessment)
8. How will you communicate with students about their work? (providing feedback)
9. What do you think you might be able to use from today's lesson to plan your next lesson? (planning using feedback and data to identify next steps)
10. How will you support the learning environment during this lesson? (knowledge of management techniques and knowledge of individual student needs)
11. What specifically would you like me to look for in this lesson? (self-knowledge; awareness of expectations, reflection)

If teachers cannot provide sufficient answers to some of these questions during the pre-observation conference, they may not have thought through the lesson with the attention necessary to address the criteria stated in the evaluation tool. It might be that a teacher has not had the time to adequately prepare for the lesson or, in some cases, does not have the knowledge and skills needed to articulate their thinking related to their teaching.

It may also be that the teacher is not familiar with the criteria identified in the evaluation tool and has not considered these components. In any case, further discussion is necessary, and principals may need to ask that more thought be given to the lesson and/or additional materials prepared. Some evaluation tool authors provide forms for teachers to complete prior to the pre-conference that guide the teacher to address specific criteria in their lesson plans. These forms may be helpful to teachers to ensure they are clear about the criteria involved in planning their lessons.

Some districts also have a specific lesson plan format that is used for planning. It is important to have some type of pre-conference guide for the discussion and to have a lens that provides language for the process. However, it should be noted that too much required pre-lesson paperwork or completion of lengthy forms can be burdensome in this time-intensive process. An effort should be made to streamline the paperwork used for the pre-conference.

Abbreviated guide sheets taken from the evaluation tool and used to facilitate lesson planning and address the criteria are most helpful, as is keeping the pre-conference brief, concise, and focused. The principal needs to ensure that the teacher is ready for the lesson observation, and that, as observer, they know what they are looking for during the observation. This means conducting the pre-observation discussion in a manner that ensures that both individuals are clear on the expectations and that teachers are given the opportunity to create a potentially successful lesson.

If a pre-conference indicates that a teacher does not seem ready to teach the lesson or has not thought through all of the criteria completely, the principal should use this time to move more deeply into the mentoring mode. Rather than using a negative response to what may seem to be a poorly planned lesson, the principal can use the information shared to suggest ideas for strengthening the plan and discuss learning goals for the teacher.

When a pre-conference indicates that more learning might be needed, an administrator can use criteria from the lens to identify what additional faculty development might be helpful. The administrator, with input from the teacher, should also determine what resources should be provided to strengthen a lesson that appears weak. They can consider whom the teacher might observe or talk with to help them expand their understanding of the criteria. In this way, the principal can support the teacher in ways that will lead to a successful lesson and observation in the near future.

Rather than continue with a process that may end up being negative, an observation can be postponed until the teacher has the opportunity to gain additional knowledge. The lesson can be refined or a new one created, using what the teacher learned in the interim. If a decision is made to proceed with an observation, the principal needs to acknowledge that they will be gathering data during the observation to validate or refute any of the concerns raised during the pre-conference discussion. In this case, a post-observation discussion will be needed to clarify both individuals' perspectives.

The purpose of any pre-observation conference is to broaden the administrator's awareness of the lesson that will be observed, but this discussion may not fully reveal the depth of the teacher's planning. While principals should use questions to help the teacher articulate the rationale for their plans, sometimes the full details of planning are not uncovered until after the lesson is taught.

The post-observation is the other necessary component of teacher support. The post-conference serves to clarify and "connect the dots" between the teacher's plans, the execution of the lesson, and the data gathered. Revisiting the pre-observation questions, or reformatting them to uncover information after the observation will help the conversation address all aspects of the lesson. This is why the full conference cycle, pre-observation, observation, and post-observation, must be completed before administrators draw any conclusions.

NOTE

1. Hattie, J. and Yates, G. C. R. (2014). *Visible Learning and the Science of How We Learn*. New York: Routledge, p. 6.

Chapter Six

Gathering Data during the Observation

Rationale for the use of data as well as options for gathering data are presented in this chapter. Multiple means of collecting data during evaluation processes are also provided. The chapter discusses how data can be a basis for supporting teacher learning and offers practice formats for this process. Pre- and post-conferences are addressed with scenarios included for practice and discussion.

Classroom observations provide data for conversations about teaching and learning. When principals are observing a class, their goal is to be unobtrusive so that what happens in the classroom is no different from what would occur if they were not present. As observers, principals need to position themselves in the classroom so that they can see both the teacher and the students. It is helpful if the administrator can avoid being constantly in the students' sight so the lesson can be seen and heard without interfering.

Usually, this means taking a seat in the back of the room, although sitting to the side is also an option. Principals can move if students are placed in groups or if the activity in the room changes location, in order to see and hear comments made by the teacher and students. Some observers prefer to remain anonymous during the observation, but students are naturally curious about having another person, especially the principal, present. It is helpful if teachers offer an introduction or brief explanation to help students view observations as a normal part of the teaching and learning process.

During the observation, principals need to gather objective, nonjudgmental data. This evidence of what is happening in the classroom is needed in order to provide feedback. At the end of the chapter is an example of an informal observation form, and several other tools that might be used to gather data during the observation. While note taking is important, mentors should not be so intent on transcribing that they fail to watch and listen carefully.

Whatever means observers use to gather evidence, the goal is to remain objective and gather specific data to help teachers examine and reflect on their practice. The observational focus can be based on a request made by a teacher who wants to gather information about a particular aspect of his or her teaching. Or, the focus can be determined by the principal's use of the identified lens/evaluation tool, with the specific criteria determined by the teacher and principal during the pre-conference discussion.

THE POST-OBSERVATION CONFERENCE

After an observation, the teacher and administrator need to get together to talk about the evidence gathered. This post-observation discussion is the ultimate opportunity to check signals and make sure the principal and teacher are on the same page regarding what was observed. It is a time to ensure that any differences in opinion about what occurred in the lesson are honestly and supportively explained and discussed.

The observation data should be shared without interpretation. The goal of the post-observation conference is to help teachers reflect on what happened in the lesson, to think about why something did or did not occur, and to consider other options or ideas for their future teaching. With early observations serving as formative assessments, the post-observation conversation is the time to set goals for the future in preparation for the next observation or the summative evaluation.

Principals serve as a mirror by using the data they gather to reflect what happened in the classroom. Teachers should lead the review of the lesson, but the principal may need to use guiding questions to assist and direct the teacher's analysis of the lesson. Such questions also can be used as a follow-up to help focus on the data and to expand the conversation beyond the teacher's initial thoughts and comments.

Based on the data gathered and the teacher's reflection on that evidence, administrators should ask their teachers what goals they would like to make regarding their work. To help teachers specifically identify how they will continue to enhance their skills, these next steps can be incorporated into observation notes, be informally noted for future reference, or used to develop an action plan. The next observational cycle should then be based upon topics identified during the post-conference.

During each subsequent observation, teachers should attempt to apply what they learned from the previous observation to the new lesson. The goal should be that by the designated time—perhaps about midterm, or during the third quarter of the year, teachers are prepared to successfully respond to a formal, summative evaluation incorporating all aspects of the lens.

In order for pre- and post-observation conferences to be effective, teachers and administrators must have developed a trusting relationship, and principals need to use effective communication skills. No matter how much data is gathered, teachers will not be able to hear or respond to suggestions if they do not trust their principal. If teachers are fearful of reprisals or negative reactions, they may not be willing to make any plans for modifying or changing their teaching.

The following scenarios can be used by administrators to practice their communication and questioning skills during pre- and post-conferences. The principal can respond to the situations either with or without using the language of a particular evaluation tool. It is beneficial to work with a colleague, with someone role-playing the teacher in the situation. If principals are not able to practice with a peer, they should write out what they might say in response to the scenario, as if they were speaking directly to that teacher, or capture their comments in a video to review.

These scenarios help principals develop a familiarity and a comfort level with the specific language and tone of their communication processes as they provide feedback. Role-playing gives administrators practice considering their responses—what they are going to say and how they are going to articulate their thoughts when responding to a teacher in a similar situation. In addition, by analyzing what is happening in the scenario, principals get practice "reading between the lines" to help interpret what a teacher is trying to say.

When administrators are in real conference settings, they have to respond, make decisions, and converse naturally. These practice scenarios provide an opportunity for principals to think about all of the options for responding to various situations and to actually state their thoughts in a pragmatic way. Practicing will enhance the principal's ability to provide immediate, nonjudgmental support in a way that encourages and invites the teacher to respond.

While there are no "right" answers for these scenarios, administrators will sharpen their own thinking skills as they try out responses and listen to how colleagues engage in the same situation. Practicing verbal responses provides principals with a chance to hear and consider their comments and to weigh the endless possibilities for the teacher's behavior. If possible, film these role-plays, as listening and watching them will enhance the learning experience. This self-analysis of communication skills will strengthen an administrator's ability to interact effectively when conferencing with their teachers.

Practice

Select a lens from chapter 4 or use your school's evaluation tool during this exercise. Apply the lens in the following pre- and post-conference scenarios, and use the observation tool as a guide for your responses. Prior to engaging in the role-play, read through the scenario descriptions below and ask yourself the following questions:

• What do you "see" and "hear" in these situations?
• What guiding questions would you ask in the conference to encourage your teacher's reflective thinking?
• Can you "ask" and not "tell" when you respond?

As you review these situations, consider the words and tone of voice needed to convey your thoughts and feelings in an honest, supportive way. In addition, review the communication process you hope to use when asking questions to probe further into what would be happening in the lesson (pre-conference) or when discussing why things occurred the way they did (post-conference).

After you have reviewed all the scenarios, select one to model. If working with colleagues, take turns playing the parts of the teacher and administrator. Multiple responses to each scenario are possible. Much of your language will depend on the evaluation tool you use and to what extent guiding questions can be incorporated into the practice session.

As the teacher, if it is appropriate for the situation, try to role-play as if you have limited understanding of your work so the principal is challenged to ask effective and probing questions. When you are the administrator in the role-play, work to generate effective questions and use appropriate communication skills. If you are writing your response, consider all the possible reasons for the teacher's behavior and describe your response.

Pre-observation Situations

1) During the pre-observation conference, the teacher seems distracted and shifts nervously in his chair. As you ask about his objectives and plans for the lesson, he mentions that he and his girlfriend have decided to get married during the winter break. You ask about the wedding plans, and then shift the conversation back to the lesson.

The teacher presents several pages of typed lesson plans and says that he hopes you will look at how he uses questioning in his class, as he thinks he might be focusing on only a few students. "Some of these fifth graders can really provide some interesting answers, and I think I am relying on only a few of the smarter ones to carry the discussion," he states. After you talk about what he has planned to do to help involve all the students in the discussion, he says that he hopes he has time to do all of this ongoing planning, "considering the approaching wedding and everything."

2) For several days you have tried to set up a time to talk with a teacher prior to today's observation. She has been busy and backed out of these scheduled meetings. She also has not responded to e-mails, so you are now talking with her during the passing period right before you are scheduled to observe the lesson. She tells you that she has everything organized, but that she will not really be teaching today as students are presenting information from their reports on explorers.

She says there really is no need for a lesson plan or conversation about the lesson prior to the observation because this is a student-centered activity. She gives you the rubric she will be using to evaluate the presentations and says that this is really a day focused on assessment and that the rubric describes what has been taught and what is expected from the students.

3) As you discuss the upcoming observation with a teacher, she refers several times to one particular student, Taylor, who really "bugs her." The lesson plan, part of a unit on healthy eating, is well planned with effective strategies for engaging all learners. Students have been recording their food intake for several days and today will compare their food journal to descriptions of healthy diets using a Venn diagram. As you conclude your conversation, the teacher says that she expects that "Taylor will not have anything done."

4) A special education teacher has planned a pull-out session for a group of four second-grade boys who are falling further and further behind in reading. She wants to give them some specific pre-reading and during-reading strategies. "It is hard to do this within the whole class in a 'push-in' model. I think I can get the boys to really focus and practice these strategies if we work alone." When you ask her about how the boys are doing in the class otherwise, she says, " They don't do their homework, even the modified work I give them, so it's hard to know how they are doing. Calls to parents have not had an effect—I just don't see much work from them."

5) A second-year middle school math teacher is using an interactive process to engage her students in the learning. She has them in groups of four at tables, and she describes to you how she has them working together on a new problem, helping each other; she then randomly selects the table group, and then one of the students in that group, to give the answer.

"This process holds them all accountable. I keep a tally of whether each group's responder is correct or not, and at the end of the unit, the group with the highest score gets five extra points on their test. The problem is, if a group falls behind and has only a few points, the team loses interest and stops trying. I am going to use this cooperative process again today, but I am not sure about how to keep my current low-scoring group motivated."

Post-Observation Situations

1) A teacher in a seventh-grade English class uses a tentative, questioning tone in all of her conversations with students. She asks them if they would like to be quiet or if they would like to start their work, and they respond by ignoring her. It takes most of the lesson just to get the students organized and working. Her lesson was to be a discussion of a novel, and the stated objective was for the students to "understand how the book's theme relates to their lives."

She put the students in groups and gave them each a chapter to talk about. No discussion guidelines were provided. She then asked students to generate ideas about the book's impact on their lives, and to have their ideas ready for tomorrow. She gave students the rest of the class to complete the work, telling them to have something written down for tomorrow because she will collect it as evidence of their work prior to the discussion.

2) A teacher in a fourth-grade classroom wanted his students to write descriptive sentences. He gave each table group a set of cards that had an adjective, a verb, or a noun printed on it and asked each group to put together the most descriptive sentence they could, using the words they were given. The groups taped their words together to create sentences and put them up on the wall for the rest of the class to see.

The students then identified the sentences they felt were the most descriptive. Following this activity, students were asked to write three descriptive sentences on their own, and share them with a table partner. The teacher asked each student to circle their best sentence and hand it in on the way out the door. All students participated except for one Latina in the back of the room.

3) The ninth-grade English class you just observed was one of the loudest you have ever witnessed. The teacher was leading a whole-class discussion on *Romeo and Juliet*. Conversations were going on throughout the lesson, several students were doing other work, and some of those who were paying attention kept saying, "This is dumb," "How do you know that is what he (Shakespeare) meant?" and "Why do we have to read this junk anyway?"

The teacher persisted, ignored all remarks, and summarized each scene. Students were asked to write a two-sentence summary before they left class, which was planned to assess their understanding of the scenes being discussed. This work was not handed in by all students. The lesson plan you discussed in the pre-conferene had seemed well organized, but the execution of the lesson will need discussion.

4) Your special education teacher was working in a fourth-grade classroom during a social studies class. Students were reading a trade book about railroads and trains, and the teacher was asking them to share any stories or experiences they had regarding trains. The special education teacher was

helping her student read sections of the text and underline and define the words he didn't know.

The student did not participate in the generation of ideas about trains, although you heard him excitedly tell the special education teacher several things he knew about trains. The student seemed eager to share, but was redirected by the teacher, who replied, "We need to focus on the vocabulary, James."

5) You have noted in previous years that a particular teacher planned lessons effectively using district materials for the grade level and subject. However, this pre-conference discussion identified her use of curriculum you are not familiar with, and you also did not see any district expectations included in her plans. You asked her to incorporate district standards into the lesson before you observed, and she agreed, without clarifying why she used the new materials.

During the post-conference, she tells you that at fall conferences, a mother who is an experienced teacher in another district, expressed concern about whether her child was successfully being engaged in the learning. The mother provided materials, directions, and suggestions to the teacher, and calls frequently to offer ideas. The teacher likes the new materials and is trying to merge both systems. She said she hoped this would be okay.

QUALITATIVE VERSUS QUANTITATIVE DATA

Administrators need to be unbiased recorders of events in a classroom. In order to identify whether a teacher has met the criteria defined in the lens/evaluation tool, there needs to be specific data gathered in relation to each component of the lens. Qualitative data gathering focuses on describing classroom interactions from a 360-degree perspective, using what the teacher and students say as the evidence.

Quantitative observation involves counting, diagramming, and more structured forms of gathering evidence. Both processes can be helpful in gathering information for teachers to consider as they think about their practice. However, qualitative observations, which focus more on open questions, are a good way to begin when a principal is first observing a teacher. Later, if more specific information is requested by the teacher, suggested by the principal or required by the evaluation tool, quantitative data can be gathered.

Written Notes and Scripting

Scripting involves taking notes about what happens during a lesson. Administrators sit in a location in the classroom that provides them with a good view of the students and the teacher and take notes on what they observe. Any mental interpreting or questioning of classroom interactions done by the observer during scripting should be noted as such so teachers have the opportunity to respond and clarify. This ensures that such interpretations are shared as thoughts, not as observed behavior.

Many evaluation tools provide a form for observers to capture what is happening in a classroom. These forms are related to the criteria and help focus the data gathering on particular areas of the teaching and learning event. However, checking a box on a form to indicate that a teacher met a criteria does not provide the evidence of what the teacher did to meet that expectation.

It is important to gather data in a scripted format prior to sitting down with a checklist and "scoring" a teacher with the evaluation tool—whether it is a formative or a summative evaluation. Without evidence to back up a checklist, the data is without substance, and a teacher may not pay much attention to it. Capturing actual language and descriptive images from the lesson in relation to the criteria on the checklist provides specific examples of what happened and should confirm any scores given.

For example, in relation to a criterion specifying the need to create a positive classroom environment, an administrator might script the following: "The teacher acted effectively during his interactions with students" or "The teacher intimidated the students with her reprimands." Both are interpretive statements. There is no identified evidence written down to support these statements, and it would be hard to argue that the teacher was really effective or if students were really intimidated. In this case, the administrator's notes are interpreting what was observed.

What principals should provide, through noninterpretive scripting and note taking, is simply a description of what occurred in the classroom. The situations might be scripted this way: "The teacher took a student aside and quietly spoke to him, after which the student began actively participating in the lesson" and "The teacher said loudly, 'Get your homework out right now! No more fooling around or I will have to keep some of you in from recess today!' Some students looked startled; all immediately took out their work." These statements are factual descriptions and are not interpretations of the events.

During a post-observation conference, considering the statement about student behavior, a principal might show the teacher his notes on the incident or read them aloud saying, "I was wondering if the students might have been a little surprised by your comments." At this point, the teacher can respond and clarify or explain the context.

Perhaps this situation was a procedure that the class had been focusing on for several weeks, and the teacher felt the students should have been able to get to work. Or the teacher might respond that she did not realize she used those particular words and an intense tone. In either case, the administrator can then ask guiding questions to facilitate the teacher's reflective thinking, such as the following:

- "How did you plan to identify those students who would be held in for recess if they hadn't gotten out their assignments?"
- "If you followed through on the consequence, how would you manage the process? Who would stay with the students who were kept in for recess? How would you manage supervision of students in two locations? Or, would you keep all of the students in for recess?"
- "Is there another way you could help students be accountable for following through on your requests?"

These questions should prompt teacher thinking. A teacher who is unable to generate answers to these questions might need more support. In this case, he or she could be given a more directive response, such as suggesting having a schedule or a daily agenda on the board so that students know when it is time to get out their homework. Or the principal could suggest that the teacher have students write the schedule on the board or in their notebooks.

Administrators can facilitate a teacher's reflective thinking by providing evidence or data from the classroom and asking him or her to respond to it. After presenting the teacher with notes identifying evidence of classroom interactions (in a supportive tone), the principal can ask follow-up questions or express thoughts, such as:

- "I was wondering what was happening with this student."
- "Why might this student have been acting this way?"
- "What was your thinking at this point?"
- "What might be the reason for this student's incorrect answer?"

Again, administrators need to avoid the urge to editorialize about why they think certain classroom interactions occurred, or to verbally point fingers at the teacher with "you" statements such as, "Why did you do that?" When administrators ask clarifying questions after an observation it gives teachers the opportunity to elaborate about their teaching.

Teachers need to be given the chance to clarify what the evidence might seem to say. This process of scripting, then discussing the qualitative data using supportive language and positive verbal tone, engages teachers in reflection about their practice.

Evidence gathered during an observation ought to be a realistic version of what occurred. Data should reflect the teacher's strengths and positive aspects of the lesson as well as areas for growth. This is the benefit of using the scripting technique—everything should be noted because the goal is to write down *all* interactions. Sharing this relatively complete overview provides a realistic image of the classroom that teachers often cannot see. The challenge for the principal is to be able to write quickly, concisely, and comprehensively, capturing on paper as much of what is happening as possible.

Observers can use several scripting formats to become proficient with gathering evidence. The adage "practice makes perfect" applies to scripting. To assist with this process, principals should try the following techniques to hone their scripting skills.

- Watch and script talk shows to develop the ability to "watch and write."
- Script a conversation that happens at home.
- Gather with several principals to observe the same TV show or videotapes of classroom interactions, without using an evaluation tool—just try to capture all events. After everyone scripts, compare each other's notes.
- Using the evaluation lens your school employees, script what you observe in relation to several criteria, while observing a video of teaching. Determine how well you captured the evidence for multiple criteria.

No matter what format is used for gathering information about a lesson, it is critical that the administrator practices writing nonjudgmental statements that only identify what was seen or heard. The conversation after the observation then can be used to "flesh out" these scripted comments as the teacher provides context and clarification.

Administrators are learning throughout the evaluation process as well, and their scripting skills may not be fully developed at the beginning of the relationship. Principals can communicate this to their teachers and ask them to help support the observer as he or she is learning. Accept the fact that scripts and notes may be less than 100 percent accurate initially and ask teachers to confirm or refute findings identified in their scripts. In this way, each individual can facilitate the other's growth and development.

VISUAL/AUDITORY EVIDENCE (I SAW . . . I HEARD . . . I THOUGHT . . .)

As it may be challenging to script and capture the full extent of classroom interactions, another effective technique is to list only what you specifically *see,* and *hear*, with a space for noting your thinking at the time. It is a good way for principals to begin gathering evidence while limiting interpretive, evaluative, or judgmental comments. This is simple and very open-ended and thus less intimidating for both parties; principals can increase their skills without having to write in such detail, and teachers are not overwhelmed by so much data.

Using the lens and asking yourself to describe only what you saw, heard, or thought in relation to a particular criteria can help focus the observation. Simply make a three-column chart and list the three statements at the top of the page, adding "in relation to _____" and fill in what you see and hear in the lesson that specifically meets the criteria. This can be a way to practice and prepare to use a formative assessment process before using a pre-designed form from an evaluation author.

Look over the examples provided in figure 6.1, and consider how you would use this information to facilitate a post-observation discussion. Discuss your response with another administrator, and give reasons for your comments. Identify why you might use a different format for different teachers or situations.

Proximity Analysis

A picture is worth a thousand words when a principal is trying to reflect what is happening in a classroom. Conducting a proximity analysis can provide teachers with an image of their movements around the classroom and among students. This diagram can help teachers become aware of the students they are focusing on and whom they are not paying as much attention to. It can be helpful for teachers to see how they are physically connecting with their students.

The use of proximity has long been considered an aid in classroom management. Most students are less likely to be off task if the teacher is standing right next to them. A description of the teacher's proximity to students in the classroom can identify which students are getting the teacher's attention. However, until you debrief, you may not know if the attention was for academic support or for maintaining positive behavior.

During the post-observation conference, after looking at the diagram from their class, teachers can consider their movements. They can think about why they moved closer to some students or did not engage others. This reflection enables teachers to identify reasons for their movements and to attune themselves to their engagement with students in the classroom.

Research has identified the importance of both the teacher's and the observer's involvement when determining what type of information will be most helpful to gather during an observation.[1] In this case, it is important to "check signals" and be sure that the teacher is aware and comfortable that a proximity analysis will be created.

To generate a proximity analysis, a diagram of the classroom is needed. A seating chart or a quick sketch of the seating arrangement will do. The drawing should identify key areas: SmartBoard, teacher's desk, and student seating. A legend should be included to identify codes used to indicate peo-

Example of scripted notes:

Name of teacher: Ms. Marks   Date: 3–12–14

Name of administrator: Mrs. Johnson   Class/grade: 10th grade Biology

Time	Scripted notes	Observers' Comments
8:45	Bell rings	Students are in seats
	Ms. M: "Today we will be looking at the process of photosynthesis. Has anyone heard this term before?" Student: "Yah, it has something to do with the plants being green." Ms. M: "Yes! What else?"	Ms. M writes student comment on board
	Students respond.	All student comments are added to list on board; M calls on 5 students—3 g (girls), 2 b (boys). Many students raise their hands, one of the boys called upon did not raise his hand.
9:00	Ms. M: "Okay! Let's take what we already know about this process and add to our info. I'd like you to take out your notebooks and write this down. Jimmy and Julie, notebooks out please."	Image of photo. (photosynthesis) process used—nice, clear diagram, on smartboard J & J (Jimmy and Julie) respond to M's request
9:15	M: "Now can anyone think of what this model looks like?" S (student): "Some sort of a factory?"	Nice use of analogy - students have to think!
	M: "Yes—a factory that produces energy for the plant and oxygen for us!"	

Example of 'hear/see/think Observation Notes:

I saw . . .	*I heard . . .*	*I thought . . .*
Becky (the teacher) watched the class start working on the assignment. She then went over to two boys and spoke to them. She then moved the boys closer together.	Becky said, "Why don't you [Joseph] and Tommy work together on the ending to the story?"	I wondered if either of these boys was struggling, and perhaps Becky put them together so that one could help the other. I wondered what the other kids would think about two students getting to work together when all of the rest had to work alone.

Figure 6.1.   Example of Scripted Notes

ple or actions in the design. The goal of a proximity analysis is to capture the teacher's movement in the classroom, indicated by an arrow and/or line.

The principal can include an indicator of teacher movement during the lesson by numbering the stops he or she makes, or perhaps by noting the duration of each pause in his or her movement. In addition, the administrator can note any other pertinent information—such as where the teacher is directing his or her comments—by drawing arrows or using some other symbol. It is helpful to note what is said to the student(s), when possible. There are no absolutes in creating a proximity diagram, except that the completed diagram should identify where the teacher was at particular moments throughout the lesson.

As with all gathered data, teachers need to put the proximity diagram into context. They need to analyze the images. Without debriefing, a proximity diagram may reflect only half of the story. For example, perhaps the teacher purposefully avoided a section of the room because students there always call out for attention, or she directed several comments toward one child because that student was absent yesterday and needed help. Unpacking the teacher's thinking in relation to how they moved and interacted in the classroom is important to ensure that the data is valid as well as helpful for the teacher.

Look over the diagram in figure 6.2. The exercise in the next paragraph provides an opportunity for administrators to reflect on what a proximity diagram says about the teaching episode.

After you review the proximity diagram, consider what the image seems to say. Think about how you would discuss this with a teacher. What patterns do you see that might need further explanation? What questions should you ask? Consider how you might begin a conversation with a teacher as you share this data. In addition, identify what misconceptions might be created without the teacher's interpretation of this diagram.

Practice creating a proximity analysis using a video to develop your comfort level with this process. If possible, share the image and your interpretation with a colleague and compare your thinking related to your analysis of the diagram. Working with a colleague helps hone the process of both gathering and sharing data from a proximity analysis and will strengthen an administrator's skills.

Numeric Data

Scripting and the use of diagrams provide evidence of classroom interactions that is qualitative and descriptive. Sometimes it is helpful for teachers to receive more specific quantitative data, and many summative evaluation tools require numeric data. Examples of numeric data might be categorizing and counting the types of questions or the number of redirecting statements a teacher utters in a class period.

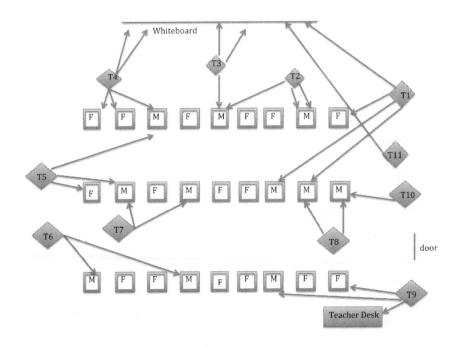

Key: T= teacher's position in the room

       T1. T2, etc., indicates the teacher's movements in the room

       ——→   Indicates the direction of the teacher's attention; where the teacher is looking

Figure 6.2.   Proximity Analysis

If a teacher uses a particular idiom or interjection in their speech that might be distracting to learners, it is helpful for administrators to identify how often this occurs. Counting the number of times a phrase occurs can be useful information for a teacher, as they may not be aware of how many times they use a speech pattern in their lessons.

The use of "like," "ya know" and "um" are examples of often unconscious interjections that can interfer with the flow of communication and distract students. While teachers may not be able to totally eliminate these phrases from their speech, being aware of them and the number of times they occur can help create an awareness of the need to provide alternate language or vocabulary.

Numeric data can also be used to identify occurrences of student behavior. A chart can be used to identify the number of students who appear to be off task at various time intervals throughout the lesson. A chart listing categories of questions might be used to keep track of how many higher level questions a teacher asks in a lesson, or perhaps to count the types of responses students make following a question. Identifying how many times something is occurring in a classroom provides insights into the interactions that impact a lesson.

Numeric evidence, which provides hard data, can feel less supportive than other forms of feedback. That is why it is important for administrators to confer with teachers about gathering this information prior to the observation. However, numeric data can be helpful when teachers are unable to reconcile what they are doing to the evidence they hear, even when previously provided with scripted data.

If principals need to be more specific and direct, numeric data can provide support for such comments. For example, if a teacher is aware of the need to ask open-ended questions to involve students in a discussion but continues to ask yes/no questions despite scripted evidence of that tendency, it would be helpful to categorize and count the types of questions being asked. With numeric data, administrators can provide evidence that a certain activity is occurring a specific number of times in a lesson. Hopefully, the teacher will see from this evidence the need to reduce or increase those behaviors.

The dialogue below allows administrators to reflect on using numeric data when observing teachers.

Dialogue — Use of Numeric Data

With another principal, discuss your comfort level with the use of numeric data, or think about the issues contained in the following questions:

1. What aspects of teaching would numeric data help you to describe?
2. When would you gather this type of evidence?
3. Is numeric data free from judgment or interpretation?
4. Could gathering numeric data impact your relationship with the teacher?

Administrators need to think about when it is appropriate to use numerical data. They should consider that gathering quantified evidence does not address the human side of the teaching act. Principals who discussed using numeric data commented that when the number of times someone does something is counted, the tally can seem to give more credence to the behavior and either validate or refute an issue. Thus, the use of numerical data needs to be focused on some aspect of teaching that can, and should, be counted.

For example, if the intent is to determine the number of times one particular student is redirected by the teacher, numerical data will identify this information. However, this data does not reflect all the other interactions that occurred during the lesson. Principals need to be clear about what they want to accomplish when gathering numerical data.

Numerical data should be gathered very intentionally and should be discussed carefully with the teacher so that the evidence supports ongoing learning. For example, if a teacher does not recognize that they are asking only lower order questions, a count of the number of open-ended questions (or lack thereof) will definitely point out this fact. It is more important, however, that this data lead to a discussion of the teacher's questioning processes and that the teacher be given resources and examples to help develop or enhance these skills.

VIDEO AND AUDIO TAPING

A digital video of a lesson provides the ultimate mirror image of the classroom. The video captures everything going on in the classroom (within range) and can help a teacher see very explicitly what is happening. Although administrators may not notice everything that goes on during a lesson or may be able to identify only certain pieces of evidence to share, the video camera records everything within its view. Teachers should be encouraged to capture their teaching on camera and reflect on it prior to being observed to self-identify their strengths as well as areas for improvement.

A video can provide the concrete evidence needed to help teachers see their teaching more clearly. Some teachers may feel comfortable sharing a video with their administrators or even watching the video together to enhance the discussion. Other teacher assessments like the edTPA for pre-service teachers and the National Board Certification process require videos of teaching episodes, so many teaches are familiar and comfortable with this process. However, it is always important for the teacher to be the one to offer to share a video.

Principals need to hone their observational skills and gather data that is helpful for teacher development. Administrators who develop a range of data-gathering skills will be able to enhance conversations with their teachers. The use of the data-gathering tools and techniques identified in this chapter can help administrators use the evaluation process to support teachers as they work to improve their skills. To be effective, discussions that focus on evidence from these data-gathering processes should be framed within the structures of good communication and a trusting environment.

NOTE

1. Glickman, C., Gordon, S., and Ross-Gordon, J. (1997). *Supervision of Instruction: A Developmental Approach* (4th edition). Boston: Allyn & Bacon.

Chapter Seven

Reflection and Goal Setting

Processes for Problem Solving and Expanding Teacher Learning

Supporting teacher reflection as a tool for educators to learn how to solve issues that occur in their classroom, and to find solutions that help their students learn, will be addressed in this chapter. Samples of reflection processes will be given that help teachers utilize evaluation feedback as a basis for ongoing learning. The use of goal setting as a tool to enhance teacher development will be discussed, and opportunities for developing responses to evaluation that enhance teacher learning are included.

Reflection is a process that is used by all effective teachers. Stepping back and considering what went well in a lesson and what might have been improved is a typical response following a teaching event. The power of reflection is that rather than assuming all went well and that students got the gist of the lesson, effective reflection processes information from the lesson in order to analyze what happened, why it happened, and what the next steps should be.

Less experienced teachers often get caught up in the events of the day and the planning needed for the next lesson and forget to take the time to reflect. It is in the reflection, when it occurs, where teachers can problem solve and identify ways to improve learning for students.

The human brain is constantly trying to solve the puzzles in our lives, and reflection provides the time to consider events and the feelings produced by these occurrences. Reflection can also provide a means to try to resolve why particular things happened. Our human brains are constantly trying to make meaning of events. Reflection is the process by which teachers make meaning from student responses and behaviors within a teaching event.

Reflection is a necessary part of any educator's path to improvement.[1] Many teachers say that this profession is one of the few careers where you "reflect on reflecting." Reflection is the professional activity that leads to action. Teachers need to think about what has happened during teaching to decide how to proceed. How do teachers know what to do next after completing a lesson? They reflect on the lesson and consider what their next action should be.

When teachers are unsure about what to do following a lesson, they might need to consider the teaching event even more carefully. By processing how a lesson unfolded, a teacher can identify what went well or what needs rethinking. They need to review any data they gathered and see what evidence they have regarding the lesson. After looking over the data, teachers will have more insight related to what students learned or didn't learn, what was effective and what didn't go as the instructor had hoped. This will help identify what teachers need to do next.

Teachers are constantly conducting experiments in their classrooms—finding ways to meet the needs of students. The questions listed below provide a process for analyzing the data from a teaching experiment—that is, the implementation of a lesson for a particular group of students on a particular day. Even if the lesson has been taught previously, a new class, a new environment can be factors, or variables, that influence the outcome of the teaching event. Reflection is a necessary part of this problem-solving processes.

Teachers need to test out practices to find those that effectively support the learning of all students as they proceed through the year. This means that teachers must engage in the use of some processes and strategies, consider the outcome and the reasons for those outcomes, and then determine the best course of action based on those reasons. This problem-solving process happens throughout the day for effective teachers.

Feedback from classroom observations provides teachers with ideas for reflection and potential change. "Receiving feedback allows the learner to close a critical gap, specifically the gap between current status and a more desirable level of achievement. . . . Feedback [is] the process of securing information enabling change through adjustment or calibration of efforts in order to bring a person closer to a well-defined goal."[2]

Data gathered during observations is vital for implementation of change. "Recent educational research suggests that objective feedback can be a powerful resource for improving teaching and learning in schools."[3] However, for feedback to be effective, it needs to focus on students' actions and behaviors in response to classroom interactions.

Reflection is most helpful for teachers when it is in response to feedback and when the thoughts are put into writing. Written reflection allows the writer a means for collecting their thoughts, reviewing events and reconsidering what happened. The reflection should be brief and descriptive and use specific language rather than employing judgmental or abstract terminology. That being said, teachers also need to think about the feedback they receive—the evidence or facts of what happened. They need to consider the reason for these events, review their reaction to the situations, and consider the students' learning.

As an administrator, it is helpful to provide options for teachers to use when they write reflections. Guiding questions can provide a structure for teachers to dig deeper into the events of a teaching episode and problem solve on their own. Principals can lead discussions with faculty about the various ways to generate reflection and use examples as a basis for practice, discussion, and faculty analysis.

There are many formats that provide a guide for reflection. These work in most situations, and usually include questions similar to the following.

Reflection question format:

What worked? What didn't work? (Identification/description)
Why did it work/Why didn't it work? (Analysis)
Which students did it work for? Who are the students for whom it did not work? (Student analysis)
What does it mean for the student/ for me? (Analysis)
How do I feel about this? (Emotional reaction/response)
What should I do next? (Action)

When working with teachers who are new to reflection or are not yet comfortable with the process, the following list of questions can be used as prompts for reflecting after a teaching episode. In addition, these are questions that a principal might use to prompt and encourage reflection following an observation.

Guiding questions/examples to consider for reflection:

1. Knowledge questions – to get at the specifics of what happened:
"Who/what/when/where/why/or how did _____ occur today?"

2. Comprehension questions – to understand and interpret events.
"Specifically describe/discuss/explain or summarize today's class or an event within the class."

3. Application questions – to help relate events to your current knowledge base.

"How were the activities in the lesson addressing the objective (or standard)?"

"What choices did I consciously (or unconsciously) make in the classroom today?"

"What were the results of those choices?"

4. Analysis questions—to develop the ability to "unpack" what happened in the lesson.

"Compare what happened in the first hour/class to what happened in the second."

"What does the students' work tell me?"

5. Synthesis questions—to put together knowledge and events.

"I wonder what might happen if I asked _____ to do _____?"

"What ideas do I have about that possible change?"

6. Evaluation questions—to identify areas of strength and areas to work on.

"What was the best thing that happened today? The most challenging?"

"What are my strengths as a teacher that I want to continue to use? What goals do I have for myself to enhance my skills?"

7. Support questions—to provide emotional support.

"How do I feel about _____?"

"What can I do/who can I talk with to get support for this issue?"

"What am I doing for fun/exercise/stress relief after work?"

8. Observation questions (using data gathered: video, audio, notes, descriptions) to help develop my ability to carefully analyze my work.

"What is happening here?" (focusing on a moment in a lesson)

"I heard/saw _____. What does that mean or indicate about the lesson?"

9. Cause/effect questions—to see the relationships between my actions (or students' actions), to the learning.

"Why do I think _____ happened?"

"What would happen if I did _____ instead?"

"What might be the reasons for _____'s behavior?"

"How could I do _____ differently?"

10. Viewpoint questions—to expand perspectives.

"How might this look to a parent/administrator/the student?"

"What might _____(student? parent?) have been thinking at that time?"

"When I saw _____, I wondered if _____ was a part of what was going on."

"What are my perspectives regarding this event?" (Allows you to pose your own "I think" comments.)

A principal's stated support for reflection is important. Teaching is challenging and difficult, and there needs to be acknowledgment of the emotional response to this work. Encouraging reflection enables the principal to support teachers' identification, expression, and perhaps resolution of emotions in a healthy way. Principals should encourage teachers to engage in this process regularly.

There are many ways an administrator can encourage teachers to reflect on their lessons. Administrators can give journals to their faculty, reinforcing the value of reflecting through the gift of a book. Principals can also adjust the schedules for their school and provide time at the end of the day for teacher and student reflection. Before students begin to pack up for the day or head off to sporting events or after-school activities, principals can institute a brief reflection time.

Playing soft music and modeling this writing activity by taking the time to jot down some thoughts on the days' events can create a culture of reflection at a school. Students can be given opportunities to learn the value of reflection and be expected to identify the positives and negatives of their daily interactions while their teachers do the same. This culture of reflection can foster deeper thinking and problem solving for both teachers and students.

Principals help make reflection a priority by holding discussions about this process, rather than just expecting reflection to occur. Administrators can share information about "framing" and "reframing"—that is, rethinking a situation and putting events into context. Discussing reflections with colleagues can help teachers see things from different perspectives. Other people's ideas about what happened regarding student work or behavior can provide a "reframe" of a situation and provide new insights and language to help address a problem.

Together, faculty and administrators can look for patterns—reviewing reflections from several courses, classes, or grade levels over time, identifying what stands out. Gathering and reviewing multiple reflections can be helpful by revealing repeated behaviors of both teachers and students. This will provide context for considering options if issues become apparent.

Providing time to share reflections with others, to come up with next steps or to analyze why something worked or didn't work, can expand a teacher's knowledge. This collaborative approach will help faculty address issues that occur in classrooms and provide for collective learning

Teachers can generate reflections in many different, less formal ways, and principals can help suggest options that support these informal reflection processes. Teachers can have a stack of Post-it notes on their desk to jot down events, student comments or thoughts "in the moment." They can keep a clipboard with students' names to write notes about how individuals are responding to lessons.

Technology can also help—using a smart phone or computer's notes section to capture thoughts following a lesson is very effective. Using a phone or camera to capture audio or video reflections can also make this process easier for busy teachers. Revisiting a reflection, whether in written, digital, or audio format is the key for teachers to be able to use the events of a lesson to examine their practice.

Principals may want to use teachers' reflections as a point of conversation in conferences before an observation. They can ask if the teachers' reflections have identified any topics they wish to discuss. This gives an administrator a means of verifying one of the key aspects of any evaluation system—the teacher's ability to engage in ongoing reflection.

Reflecting is an indicator of an educator's efforts to meet the ongoing needs of students. However, it can be hard to tell how effectively a teacher reflects during a conference. Asking teachers to comment on events following an observation provides another way for administrators to hear some of the teacher's reflective thinking. However, reflection is not instantaneous, and some time is often needed to carefully consider recent events. Revisiting a lesson later, taking time to consider what happened and why it happened, helps teachers process the event and find answers.

Because reflection doesn't happen instantaneously, principals need to provide time for this thinking. By encouraging a process and providing options and discussions about reflection, administrators can facilitate the development of effective reflective practices that foster ongoing problem-solving skills. Supporting the wide use of reflection, giving teachers time to work with colleagues, to analyze events identified in their reflections and come up with options for addressing issues or concerns, provides a means for educators to be self-directive about their personal development.

GOAL SETTING TO EXPAND LEARNING

As educators hone their ability to reflect and analyze their teaching, principals can encourage faculty to set goals to address issues that surface. When teachers recognize from reflections and conversations with colleagues the areas of their teaching they want to address, the next step is setting some personal goals. Using the evaluation tool as a guide to identify the specific aspects of effective teaching they wish to address can help teachers plan for their own development.

The language of the evaluation tool can provide a specific focus for a teacher's goal. It is helpful for principals to guide this self-learning by providing a format for teacher goal setting. A format that uses data gathered by the teacher, self-reflection statements, and criteria from the evaluation tool will provide a means for creating personal development plans. Teachers who develop and share such plans with an administrator are identifying their efforts to improve their skills and their students' learning.

Teachers will respond to requests to develop goal-setting plans more readily if a principal has built trust among faculty members. If teachers do not choose to set goals for themselves, do not find their reflections or discussions provide insight into their teaching, or do not identify areas to continue to learn, the principal needs to offer assistance. When teachers are unable to identify ongoing learning for themselves, the use of goal-setting formats can help.

If reflection is encouraged and modeled by the administrator, most teachers will develop the ability to self-analyze and establish goals for themselves. If this does not happen, principals need to set the expectation that there will be ongoing learning. Principals also need to ensure that goals set by teachers are measurable and attainable, and that there are resources available to support the teacher's work toward these goals.

Figures 7.1 and 7.2 show examples of an action plan that can be used to facilitate teacher development and goal setting. The teacher and administrator should complete the forms together and discuss the plan as a part of an observation post-conference.

This example of a completed action plan addresses how a teacher is taking steps to respond to negative student behavior. By identifying a process that includes resources and next steps, a principal can support a teacher's learning and assist them as they set goals and work to solve a classroom problem.

Issue or behavior concern	Strategies to address the situation	Teacher Goal(s)	Resources	Timeline	Reflection questions
Information identifying the specific classroom issue or behavior:					
Next steps based on information gathered in initial steps:					

Signed: _____   _____   _____
(Principal)   (Teacher)   (date)

Figure 7.1.

Practice Action Plan

Consider the issue listed in the action plan in figure 7.3, and make suggestions as if you were helping a teacher create and implement this plan in a post-observation setting. Consider your language, tone, and knowledge of strategies and resources. Try using other issues or behaviors from your own experience that you may need to address with a faculty member to practice developing these plans. Work with a colleague and think about all the ways you could support the teacher's ongoing learning around this issue.

Here is a process that can be used to set up an action plan and identify teacher goals:

1. Identify the issue, using data from an evaluation, observation, or reflection.
2. Briefly describe what the teacher is currently doing in relation to this situation, based on discussion, data, and reflections.
3. Identify resources to read/gather in order to learn more about the situation.
4. List one or two goals for continued learning in this area.
5. Identify a strategy or plan or steps to implement.
6. Estimate time frame for implementation.
7. Complete suggested readings/ implement strategy.
8. Identify next steps that respond to initial data gathering or actions.
9. Summarize effects/results of implementation.

Issue or behavior concern	*Teacher Goal(s)*	*Strategies to address the situation*	*Resources*	*Timeline*	*Reflection questions*
Information identifying issue: Mary, a third- grade student, is constantly shouting out answers, talking very loudly in class when not called on, and disturbing her classmates. Her fellow students do not want to include her in their play, so Mary forces her way into their games.	1. To develop a calmer response to the student's off-task behavior 2. To develop a deeper understanding of the reasons why Maary, and other children may resort to loud and interupting behviors	1. Check Mary's file or talk to her first- and second- grade teachers to determine if this pattern occurred in previous years. 2. Read about similar behaviors (see resources) 3. Talk to the special-education teacher	Provide resource for teacher to read: *Causes & Cures in the classroom: Getting to the root of academic and behavior problems* Searle, M. (2013), Alesandria, VA: ASCD.	1. Reading from the resource completed & discussed next week in PLC _____ (date). 2. Additional reading completed by next observation meeting _____ (date)	Am I meeting my goals? Am I finding ways to be more supportive? Do I know more about what causes this type of behavior?
Follow up based on information gathered in initial steps:		4. Implement behavior strategies based on the success of previous teachers and readings. 5. Monitor a behavior plan for success 6. Keep data on the number of times Mary disturbs class or playmates for the three weeks	2.Share/ discuss the book in PLC and look for ideas to use in the classroom. 3. Reflect and monitor effectiveness of new ideas.	3. Start Monday _____ (date). 4. Facilitate a three-week behavior plan. 5. Gather data 6. Review data and determine next steps.	

Signed: _____   _____ _____
        (Principal)   (Teacher)   (date)

Figure 7.2.

Issue or behavior concern	Teacher Goal(s)	Strategies to address the situation	Resources	Timeline	Reflection questions
Student doesn't do homework and is failing because of it. Parents are concerned but have no suggestions. Class grade includes homework as 50% of the final grade.					
Next steps:					

Signed: _____ _____ _____

         (Principal)   (Teacher)   (date)

Figure 7.3.

Principals may want to provide a structured approach such as this to show how teachers can continue to grow and develop their skills. When a teacher and administrator develop ways to enhance what is happening in a class-room—from the use of teaching and learning strategies, to classroom management issues, to choices of curriculum—and set up an action plan, there is a process in place that provides clarity of expectations.

Administrators may negotiate the selection of goals with the teacher, but self-selected goals will be the most meaningful for teachers to pursue. The identification of an issue that is challenging the teacher is a good place to begin when writing an action plan. There can be no "got ya" situations if everyone has clearly identified the goals, resources are provided to help the teacher meet the goal, and results are shared and discussed. The use of these processes is a way to make sure that teachers and principals are on the same page when it comes to addressing ongoing learning goals.

NOTES

1. Schon, D. (1990). *Educating the Reflective Practitioner.* San Francisco: Jossey-Bass.

2. Hattie, J. and Yates, G. C. R. (2014). *Visible Learning and the Science of How We Learn.* New York: Routledge, p. 6.

3. Gerald, C. (2012). *Ensuring Accurate Feedback from Observations.* Bill & Melinda Gates Foundation, p. 9.

Chapter Eight

Resources and Practices Necessary for Success

What opportunities should administrators provide teachers to support their ongoing development? What resources do principals need to provide for teachers that will enhance students' learning? This chapter identifies resources and practices that will enhance effective evaluation processes and enable a positive environment to flourish in a school community.

What is needed for principals to successfully guide a faculty through evaluation processes that expand and enhance teacher development? Mentoring practices have long identified these components, and administrators who establish school-wide practices to support and incorporate these resources will find greater success in guiding teacher development. These are key components that should be in place or added to the school environment by the principal in order to facilitate an effective support and evaluation process.

CONFIDENTIALITY

Before beginning any evaluation and support process, confidentiality must be discussed. This is vital to the success of the process. If the principal is providing formative assessments and mentor-like support, teachers need to be assured that access to data related to prior observations and early evaluations will not be shared with anyone. "Putting on the mentor hat" is an important "frame" for any formative evaluation.

Teachers need to know that this is a learning process and that there will be no negative repercussions from early observations. The formative assessment data should be "owned" by the teacher to use as they continue to hone their skills. Principals do not keep the forms or any notes from early observations, but should hand over any data to the teacher. The only data that is kept by administrators is from the final summative evaluation. The principal needs to try and set any earlier perceptions aside when conducting a summative evaluation so that the observer sees the teacher "in the moment."

For administrators to incorporate a mentoring and support component into evaluation processes, there has to be a clear break between what happens prior to the final evaluation and that summative event. Administrators need to document and score only what happens in the final evaluation. There should be no comparisons or connections to what was observed previously.

This process needs to be specifically defined so teachers are clear about the separation between each evaluation. Teachers should be encouraged to identify what they are working on and define their growth over time during the final evaluation conference; however, it is the teacher who owns the earlier data and it is their choice to identify what (if any) earlier data to discuss. While it is challenging for the principal, the ability to separate and look only at the teaching events and data from the final evaluation is critical to creating an environment where teachers are willing to use evaluation data to improve.

STRUCTURE AND FUNDING

Principals need to develop structures within the school if they want to support a mentoring approach to the evaluation process. They need to be able to provide the resources, financial and otherwise, necessary for the program's success.

In addition, a principal who wants to support teachers and help them improve, rather than just generating a "score," will find it difficult to do so alone. Creating a support team can be an important structure for effective evaluation processes. Selecting teachers to be mentors or peer coaches expands the options for observations. In some cases, hiring outside mentors may be necessary. A system of support provided by multiple individuals can be helpful, as long as these individuals have also been involved in building trust and developing effective communication.

When selecting faculty for the support team, it is often comfortable for a principal to choose faculty who hold similar perspectives regarding evaluation. However, gathering a team of diverse individuals can be an asset. Selecting individuals who can bring multiple perspectives to the evaluation process will help expand the ways in which observations and data are interpreted.

A team with a range of visions and perspectives will help teachers recognize that they are not being subjected to just one person's reaction to their work. Using a team of peer mentors/coaches helps provide multiple perspectives regarding evaluation data. While some might find it more supportive to have the same person conduct observations across the year, having a choice of mentors can also be reassuring to teachers.

Allowing teachers to select who they want to be their mentor/observer helps create a positive process. Even better, training all teachers in mentoring skills will enable everyone in the school to be a peer mentor and observer. Teachers who are able to work together, observe each other and provide feedback, create a climate that supports ongoing learning, manages the system, and minimizes financial aspects of this process.

However, the principal must set the tone for this engagement and be a part of the formative observation structure. Putting this support totally in faculty mentors' hands removes the principal from the process. If the principal is not a part of the mentor team, it can undermine the administration's attempt to create an environment where everyone is working to improve.

A timeline and framework for when observations will happen and how pre- and post-observation discussions will occur also needs to be established. There should be designated places where teachers can meet and talk and, hopefully, a process for providing substitute teachers to facilitate peer observations. Because this structure for effective support of teacher development and evaluation may need additional financial resources to implement, it is critical that school district budgets include the necessary funds.

It is a reality that school finances will impact this process, but success with the evaluation process requires monetary support. If funding is not available for outside speakers, training, additional mentors, or stipends for peer coaching, principals may need to ask the faculty to share this work as in-house experts. Providing opportunities for nonevaluative peer observations, where teachers can choose to watch each other and then chat about their work, can be a helpful and less costly process.

However, if teachers are working together to enhance their skills, release time and financial support (stipends) are an important validation of these efforts. Administrators need to creatively rotate faculty release time and manage funding to provide time for observations and stipends for faculty observers, in order to ensure success.

The financial implications for an effective evaluation support process are a challenge for many schools and districts. Financial structures must be identified and put into place to allow administrators to facilitate such evaluation models. School boards need to be provided information to help them focus budgets on funding evaluation systems in order to improve and increase student achievement.

DATA AND PROCESSES

There needs to be clarity around the use of data and the sequence of events surrounding the evaluation process. Teachers need to know that the system is not a "got you" process—that the goal is indeed about improvement to support student learning. The principal needs to communicate that the evaluation process is focused on teacher development. Clear, specific timelines and expectations need to be communicated. This is a part of the structure or framework of the evaluation process.

School board and legislature decisions send messages to teachers, and hopefully these decision-making bodies will recognize the value of incorporating support within the evaluation process. It is most helpful if the data required by a state or district focuses on growth.

Regardless of the evaluation tool used, administrators and school boards need to identify the rationale for the evaluation and the required outcome and data-collection process. There are many questions that need to be answered in order to establish a process that is comfortable for all involved. For example:

- How will teachers be given opportunities to learn what is expected before the evaluations begin?
- When will initial formative observations occur? And will these observations be followed by adequate opportunities for faculty to address areas for development?
- How will teachers' areas of strengths be validated and communicated to the school community?
- How many observations and support opportunities are provided prior to the formal evaluation?
- How will observations be scheduled and who else, besides the principal, will be working with teachers?
- Are there only scheduled observations, or are some observations unannounced?
- What final-score level will be required for teachers to be identified as "proficient"?
- Where is final evaluation data kept and who has access to it?
- Is there a score, or set of scores, from the final summative evaluation that will trigger remediation? When would this remediation process be initiated? What does remediation entail?
- What are the "next steps" following a successful evaluation?
- Can teacher evaluation data be gathered for several years, with a trend line identified to show each teacher's growth over time?

All of these questions, and undoubtedly others that will be raised by those involved, must be answered adequately before any evaluation process can be implemented. If there are still uncertainties related to the evaluation process and use of data collected, teachers will be hesitant to participate. Clarity about expectations and definitive processes is absolutely necessary to ensure that everyone involved in the evaluation process is on the same page.

TIME

Any effective process takes time. For an evaluation process to provide accurate information, administrators need to have the time to accomplish the associated tasks. How many times will faculty be observed? Will these observations be structured (with a pre- and post-conference included) or will these observations be informal? School districts will need to consider these issues prior to implementing any teacher assessment process.

The number of observations required impacts time. If there are two or three formative observations required and one summative assessment for every teacher in the school, this must be factored into the decisions regarding the implementation of the teacher assessment. The number of faculty members who will be a part of this process is a major factor in providing appropriate time in order for this support system to work. A principal must be able to adequately divide up his or her time in order to complete the observations and conferences as well as support faculty development related to the evaluation.

School districts need to identify how to create this time. Providing a schedule to support this work is one way to ensure that all teachers will be given adequate time to meet the expectations for the evaluation. Utilizing assistant principals, teachers on special assignment, peer coaches, or outside mentors are all possible ways to add time to support this process. These individuals will need flexible schedules that allow for observing and discussing teaching during the formative evaluations.

There are valid concerns related to how much time is given to an observation or what options are available for connecting with teachers. It would be a concern if administrators popped in and used very brief moments in the class and called that a full observation, or if administrators did not consider the issues and alterations that can occur in a teacher's schedule.

Another way to address the issue of time is to plan the number of observations carefully. How many interactions are needed to guide the formative process effectively? If the principal makes only one formative observation, followed up by learning opportunities and support by mentors, and then conducts one final summative evaluation—would this be adequate? The key is the amount of support and number of learning opportunities provided for teachers to address any issues raised in the first observation.

An administrator might consider the possibility of hiring a manager to conduct office tasks in order to free the principal to focus on evaluations. If the resource of time is not provided, it is highly unlikely that the evaluation process will be supportive or effective for teacher growth. While individuals in authority may be eager to implement a teacher evaluation process quickly, if the time is not given to create a process that reflects appropriate opportunities to develop and grow, then the teachers may be fearful and noncompliant.

ACCESS TO CONTENT AND INSTRUCTIONAL RESOURCES

Whether planning processes need to be defined, management practices investigated, or new content explored, teachers need to have access to resources in order continue to learn and grow in these areas. They cannot be expected to implement what they do not know. While some administrators may think that these best practices should already be incorporated into a teachers' skill set, it is not necessarily the case.

If the expectation is for teachers to meet every aspect of an identified teacher evaluation tool, then the administrator must provide opportunities for faculty to learn and understand every one of the criteria articulated in the tool. This learning may be in the form of in-school faculty development experiences provided for everyone or may be opportunities for teachers to attend workshops and conferences related to the particular area they wish to strengthen.

While administrators probably do not have expertise in all aspects of the evaluation tool being used with teachers, the principal's credibility rests on their ability to speak knowledgeably about the expectations for teachers. It is important that administrators participate in training themselves to make sure they clearly know what each aspect of the evaluation tool "looks like" and "sounds like" when employed by a teacher. This is vital in order to provide knowledgeable, insightful feedback during formative assessments as well as valid, reliable, and fair responses on the final evaluation.

Administrators need to be a part of any training and workshops provided for the teachers on campus. Learning and working together sends a powerful message. An administrator who shows that he or she also will be learning, positions him or herself as someone who is on the same team as the faculty in preparing to successfully meet the expectations of the evaluation.

If possible, the administrator should also undergo a rigorous evaluation that involves teacher input. It will be difficult to expect teachers to listen to feedback from someone who does not engage in the same processes. Early on, establish the fact that addressing the expectations of the evaluation is something everyone, including the principal, will be doing this year.

It is important to create a team-learning environment when teachers are working to strengthen their knowledge and skills. Using PLCs (professional learning communities) to organize teachers into logical groups is one way to structure this process. The principal should be on a team with other school administrators during any learning event or workshop.

Principals need to work alongside their faculty members, considering how the language of the tool is represented in classroom activities, teacher work, and student responses. This is not a time to be a lone wolf. Teachers and administrators need to collaborate to share ideas and to create a sense of common understanding of what is expected of teachers in the evaluation tool and what areas need additional opportunities for learning. Sharing and using resources, followed by time for personal reflection and then group discussion, is an effective structure to employ during these learning events.

Confidentiality, structure and resources, data and processes, as well as access to content and instructional resources are important aspects of any supportive evaluation system. An administrator may have developed a positive environment and honed his or her communication skills, but these components also need to be addressed to provide a well-structured system that leads to teacher development. The goal should always be to foster teacher knowledge and skills in a supportive way to increase teacher effectiveness and enhance student learning.

Chapter Nine

Strengthening Skills

This chapter will provide situations that enable principals and administrators to practice their response to teachers regarding evaluation processes and resulting issues. A range of options for practice is provided that allow current and developing administrators to focus on the language and response to various situations. Practicing responses to these scenarios and reflecting with colleagues will develop effective support processes.

Principals who want to develop communication skills and support teachers' ongoing learning need to practice these kinds of interactions. To use mentoring skills effectively, an administrator needs to take the time to consider effective ways to respond to teachers, particularly in challenging situations.

The following scenarios provide opportunities to consider the language and tone of your conversations and use the vocabulary of the evaluation tool adopted by your district. In addition, consider what information you need in order to construct an effective reply to your teachers. Is there a need for an action plan? Adjust the scenario to fit your particular setting to help make your response as realistic as possible.

If possible, work with a colleague or use a video camera to capture your response. This will provide opportunities to reflect on your ability to provide supportive feedback. Try formulating responses to multiple scenarios, focusing on different aspects of your communication and alternative options for the teacher. Consider how you can work to improve your interactions with faculty. Your ultimate goal should be to create supportive environments that generate positive evaluation systems and teacher growth so that student learning is positively impacted.

SITUATIONS FOR PRINCIPALS TO PRACTICE MENTORING RESPONSES

1) Your school has a monthly assessment used to identify how students are progressing in their learning. However, the teacher you are talking with does not feel that this test is an accurate representation of what she is teaching or of what the students are learning. All team members are supposed to use this assessment.

The teacher does not agree that this instrument should be used. Her students do not do well on the assessments, yet she claims they are learning. Assessments are a large part of the teacher evaluation process that you are implementing. How do you respond in a way that keeps the relationship positive? How do you help this teacher embrace the monthly assessment? (Or do you?) Specifically, what will you say? What information do you share? What do you ask?

2) You have many students who come to your school with a limited educational background. Your last faculty meeting focused on engaging students in lessons, a major component of your teacher evaluation tool. You have just watched a lesson where students were constantly, in strongly worded commands, told to sit still, be quiet, and listen to the teacher.

Students do engage in the completion of an assignment with a partner. You noted compliance on the part of the students, but also felt a sense of tension in the room. In your post-conference, the teacher states that she has worked hard to provide structure for her students and keep them focused because they do not know how to "do school." Your response?

3) The physical education teacher has planned a culminating tournament following a unit on badminton. When you ask about how he is organizing the games, he says, "I want all the kids to be challenged to play well, but there are some kids who really are awful and some who excel in the game. At first I thought about mixing up the ability levels in each team, but I didn't want some of the more athletic kids to get frustrated with teammates who miss returns or serves. I figured that it might be good to put kids of similar ability together to challenge them and so they won't get irritated with one another. I could tell you right now which teams will be in the final match—not all of them will do well, but at least everyone is going to be playing on a team where they will be able to participate equally. I'm just not sure this is the best way to structure this tournament." What is your response, considering your school's goal to focus on helping all students succeed?

4) A teacher spends a lot of time developing a hallway bulletin board and creative images to exhibit in her room. She won a prize in past years for the environment in her classroom. However, this teacher also feels she does not have sufficient time to complete all the demands of teaching, such as lesson planning, data tracking, and adapting lessons for her English language learn-

ers. You have noted the lovely classroom and are now debriefing a lesson that was less than stellar. How do you begin this conversation? What evidence will you want to gather to support goal setting for this teacher?

5) You observe a teacher's classroom where a student repeatedly talks out of turn, talks back to the teacher, disrupts lessons, disrespects the teacher and other students, and does not do her work. You hear that the teacher has tried to contact the parent, but the single mother can't be reached, as she works the night shift and sleeps during the day. The teacher has given low grades to the student to reflect the behavior issues that erupt in the classroom.

You witnessed the child's behavior as well as the teacher's efforts to positively shape the student's behavior. As the principal, you want to provide assistance but are also concerned because behavior has been incorporated into the student's evaluation and grade, and you wonder about the student's academic work. How do you shape your conversation with this teacher?

6) Your school has identified a planning process to be used for generating effective lessons, and faculty members have been discussing the required components. The process and format reflect the expectations in your approved teacher evaluation tool. However, one senior teacher feels that taking the time to write down plans is not necessary as he "carries all his effective lessons in his head." His lessons are pretty good, but all faculty will be assessed using the evaluation tool. After observing and seeing only notes—not the prescribed lesson plan format, what do you say?

7) A teacher wonders about what process to use to help motivate her students to try their best, pay attention in class, and complete their work. She is constantly talking to students about the impact of doing well in school so they will have a brighter future. This has not been successful, so she is looking for something that will enable her to provide a connection to doing well in school and her students' future. You heard her articulate these encouragements in her classroom, and now as you conduct your post-conference, you need to decide how to address this concern and provide ideas and support.

8) Observing a first-year teacher early in the year, you recognize that there is too much chaos in the room. During your pre-conference, the teacher said her students needed to learn how to "be" in school. She wants to spend more time focusing on building relationships, establishing routines and procedures, and creating a classroom community.

However, she also wants academics to be the focus, as weekly tests are required as a means of identifying student growth. The teacher feels she must work on academics to come up with good weekly scores, even though she thinks building a community would help in the long run. She is frustrated and sad, almost tearing up as you speak. You observed a strong lesson, even though the students were disruptive. How do you address this issue? What supports do you offer?

9) You have reviewed with your faculty the evaluation tool that your district has adopted. This instrument asks that teachers work to provide lessons that engage their students in higher level thinking. You are observing and note that this lesson has lots of good questions offered by the teacher, but that only a few students respond. The teacher says "Good!" or "Nice job!" every time a student answers.

You want to help the teacher move to a point where all students are involved and discussing the topic at a deeper level and not engaged in such a teacher-directed question-and-answer format. You want to validate the efforts the teacher has made in developing the questions that were included in the lesson plan, but you think this could be more student centered. How do you facilitate this conversation?

10) Your social studies teachers are examining student work in their PLCs. The feedback to students on assignments is limited to check marks for incorrect answers on a multiple-choice test. The teachers do have a rubric to use with essay questions and are talking about creating a list of responses that they can provide electronically to students after each essay test. You have reviewed the *"provide clear feedback to students to support their ongoing learning"* part of your evaluation tool with them at a previous PLC. You sit down with them—what do you say to help them move forward?

11) A teacher has been exceptional with whole-class instruction. You would like him to try to incorporate some cooperative learning into his teaching, having stated in a pre-conference that expectations for engaged learning are a part of your school's evaluation tool. You have shared and discussed several articles on the subject, and after your last observation, the teacher identified a goal to use some cooperative learning strategies in future lessons. As you talk with him about the lesson you will be observing today, you note that it is, again, a whole-class lesson. What do you focus on in this conversation?

12) The tenth-grade choir was rehearsing a new song. While the teacher worked with the sopranos, the rest of the class talked loudly, sometimes tossing things at each other across the room. The teacher repeatedly turned and told the class to be quiet, saying that they needed to be respectful while one of the sections was working and that they should be looking over their music. A few seconds after each reprimand, the class was back chatting as loudly as before. This went on all lesson long, whenever the teacher worked separately with a group on a difficult section of the music.

13) You have been working with all your teachers for several weeks, asking them to clarify what they would like to focus on from the evaluation tool that you will be using as a formative assessment during a later visit. Today is your first visit to a second-grade teacher's class. As you discuss the upcoming observation, the teacher says, "I really want to be more clear with

my directions. I think that I often say things in a somewhat confusing way, so my struggling students don't know what to do."

You tell him that you will look closely at this and see if you can gather some information on the clarity of his directions. You note that he has tested and divided his students by reading ability. You ask him how he came to this decision. He replies that he really likes reading groups because it is easier to address the common needs of students rather than worry about all of them at once. He adds that he does not use these groups all the time. What do you discuss when you have your post-observation visit?

14) The kindergarten class you observed was listening to a story, with the goal of having students predict what would happen next. The teacher read with an enthusiastic tone, and most students seemed to be focused and listening. Whenever the teacher stopped, she repeatedly called on one of three students to make a prediction, despite the fact that other children raised their hands to answer.

15) A high school science teacher assigned her students a reading from a text that describes plant and animal cells and includes directions for a cell exploration lab. This reading was given the night before in a "flipped classroom" model. During class, she gave her students leaf samples and told them to follow the directions in the text and then write up a lab report on their findings. Most students followed the directions and correctly created slides of plant cells.

They also created another slide, using scrapings taken from inside their mouths. When this was done, students were then told to examine these slides under a microscope and identify the similarities and differences between the two cell types, using the text and their lab results to support their answers. Students were given a template for the lab report that asked them to draw the cells as they saw them through the microscope. You noticed that some students seemed to be struggling with the reading and worked more slowly than others.

16) At the end of the second trimester, a teacher reviews student math placement tests and finds that he scored one student's test incorrectly. He realizes that the student should have been in the accelerated math program since the beginning of the year. He is nervous about talking to you, has not talked to the parent about this and would like to avoid the issue altogether. Still, he knows it would not be fair to the student to ignore this information. He tells you the whole story during a post-observation conference and, somewhat fearfully, asks what he should do. What do you say?

17) As you observe a class, a teacher is trying to manage a behavior situation in the classroom when one of the students calls the teacher a racist. The teacher is clearly upset by this and doesn't know what to say, so she ignores the comment, even thought it was obviously heard by everyone in the

junior high classroom. When you meet to talk about the lesson, she immediately asks, "What should I do about that comment??!!" What do you say?

18) A sixth-grade math teacher asked his students to create a survey to gather data to be displayed in a graph. The students decided to ask their classmates about their favorite school lunch items and created several questions to ask them at lunch. During this lesson, students graphed their results. Their work included some graphs that had tally marks for all responses, some with averages, some with comparisons. There were pie charts, bar graphs, and line graphs.

Before the students began working on their graphs for today's class, the teacher told them they needed to use the most appropriate method to clearly display their results. Students responded effectively and produced quality work. After the teacher collected the graphs, he told the students that they were also going to be graded on neatness. Provide your feedback and comments, particularly focused on assessment, using the evaluation tool that your district has endorsed.

19) The lesson you just observed did not go well. The technology would not work, some students were not prepared—they had not read the text, and directions on student materials were unclear. The plan stated that there would be a video shown that provided a counterpoint to the assigned reading. The students were to watch, then respond to both resources in writing, taking a position on a particular topic or event. Without the video, the teacher just said to write a paragraph on what they read, exchange with a partner, and provide feedback. Students kept asking for clarification about what they should write about without the video to contrast with the text.

20) You have directed your teachers to focus on the "*helping students develop and test hypothesis*" part of the evaluation tool your school uses. A math teacher comes to you and asks how she should do this. "I teach the students the math heuristic and we practice it and I test them. They cannot formulate a hypothesis in math—that is a science concept. Math formulas are already established. Students need to learn them, know when to use them, and calculate their answers." What do you say?

Resources

Barrett, J. (2000). Relationships. In M. Boushel, M. Fawcett, and J. Selwyn (Eds.), *Focus on Early Childhood.* Oxford: Blackwell Science.

Bennis, W., and Nanus, B. (2003). *Leaders: The Strategies for Taking Charge.* New York: HarperCollins.

Blake, S. (1999). At the crossroads of race and gender: Lessons from the mentoring experiences of professional black women. In A. Murrell, F. Crosby, and R. Ely (Eds.), *Mentoring Dilemmas: Developing Relationships within Multicultural Organizations* (83–104). Mahwah, NJ: Lawrence Erlbaum Associates.

Bolman, L. and Deal, T. (1992). Leading and managing: Effects of context, culture and gender. *Education Administration Quarterly* 28, 314–29.

Bouquillon, E., Sosik, J., and Lee, D. (2005). "It's only a phase": Examining trust, identification and mentoring functions received across the mentoring phases. *Mentoring and Tutoring* 13(2), 239–58.

Brookhart, S. (2008). *How to Give Effective Feedback to Your Students.* Alexandria, VA: ASCD.

Brooks, V. (2000). School-based initial teacher training: Squeezing a quart into a pint pot or a square peg into a round hole? *Mentoring and Tutoring* 8(2), 99–112.

Butler, T, and Chao, T. (2001). Partners for change: Students as effective technology mentors. *Active Learning in Higher Education* 2(2), 101–13.

Chapel, S. (2003). Responsibilities of subject mentors, professional mentors and link tutors in secondary physical education initial teacher education. *Mentoring and Tutoring* 11(2), 131–51.

Cobb, A., Stephens, C., and Watson, G. (2001). Beyond structure: The role of social accounts in implementing ideal control. *Human Relations* 54(9), 1123–53.

Cuddapah, J. (2002). The teachers college new teacher institute: Supporting new teachers through mentoring relationships. Paper presented at the annual meeting of the American Educational Research Association. (ERIC Document Reproduction Services no. ED 470683)

Danielson, C. (1996). *Enhancing Professional Practice: A Framework for Teaching.* Alexandria, VA: Association for Supervision and Curriculum Development.

Danielson, C. (2011). *The Framework for Teaching Evaluation Instrument.* Princeton, NJ: The Danielson Group. http://www.danielsongroup.org.

Danielson, C., and McGreal, T. (2000). *Teacher Evaluation to Enhance Professional Practice.* Princeton, NJ: Educational Testing Service.

Daresh, J. (2002). *Teachers Mentoring Teachers.* Thousand Oaks, CA: Corwin.

Darling-Hammond, L. (2013) *Getting Teacher Evaluation Right: What Really Matters for Effectiveness and Improvement.* New York: Teachers College Press.

Darling-Hammond, L. (2003). Keeping good teachers: Why it matters what leaders can do. *Educational Leadership* 60(8), 6–13.

Delgado, M. (1999). Developing competent practitioners. *Educational Leadership* 56(8), 45–48.

Dindia, K. (2000). Self-disclosure, identity and relationship development: A dialectical perspective. In K. Dindia and S. Duck (Eds.), *Communication and Personal Relationships.* Chichester, UK: Wiley.

Dindia, K., and Duck, S. (Eds.) (2000). *Communication and Personal Relationships.* Chichester, UK: Wiley.

DuFour, R. (May 2004). What is a Professional Learning Community? *Educational Leadership*, 61(8), 6–11.

Dweck, C. (2006). *Mindset: The New Psychology of Success.* New York: Ballantine Books.

Evertson, C., and Smithey, M. (2000). Mentoring effects on protégés' classroom practice: An experimental field study. *Journal of Educational Research* 93(5), 294–304.

Fabian, H., and Simpson, A. (2002). Mentoring the experienced teacher. *Mentoring and Tutoring* 10(2), 117–25.

Feiman-Nemser, S. (April, 2001). Combining assistance and formative assessment: The case of the Santa Cruz New Teacher Project. Paper presented at the annual meeting of the American Educational Research Association, Seattle, WA.

Feiman-Nemser, S. (2003). What new teachers need to learn. *Educational Leadership* 60(8), 25–29.

Feiman-Nemser, S., Carver, C., Schwille, S., and Yusko, B. (1999). Beyond support: Taking new teachers seriously as learners. In M. Scherer (Ed.), *A Better Beginning: Supporting and Mentoring New Teachers* (3–12). Alexandria, VA: ASCD.

Fideler, E., and Haselkorn, D. (1999). *Learning the Ropes: Urban Teacher Induction Programs and Practices in the United States.* Belmont, MA: Recruiting New Teachers.

Garvey, B., and Alred, G. (2000). Educating mentors. *Mentoring and Tutoring* 8(2), 113–26.

Geen, A., Bassett, P., and Douglas, L. (1999). The role of the secondary school subject mentor: An evaluation of the UWIC experience. *Mentoring and Tutoring* 7(1), 55–65.

Gerald, C. (2012). *Ensuring Accurate Feedback from Observations.* Seattle: Bill and Melinda Gates Foundation.

Giebelhaus, C., and Bowman, C. (2000). Teaching mentors: Is it worth the effort? Paper presented at the Annual Meeting of the Association of Teacher Educators, Orlando, FL. (ERIC Document Reproduction Services no. ED 438277).

Gilbert, L. (2005). What helps beginning teachers? *Educational Leadership* 62(8), 36–39.

Gilles, C., Cramer, M., and Hwang-Lee, S. (2001). New teacher perceptions of concerns: A longitudinal look at teacher development. *Action in Teacher Education* 23(3), 92–96.

Gilles, C., and Wilson, J. (2004). Receiving as well as giving: Mentors' perceptions of their professional development in one teacher induction program. *Mentoring and Teaching* 12(1), 87–106.

Glickman, C., Gordon, S., and Ross-Gordon, J. (1997). *Supervision of Instruction: A Developmental Approach* (4th edition). Boston: Allyn & Bacon.

Gold, Y. (1992). Psychological support for mentors and beginning teachers: A critical dimension. In T. Bey and C. Holmes (Eds.), *Mentoring: Contemporary Principles and Issues.* Reston, VA: Association of Teacher Educators.

Goleman, D. (1995). *Emotional Intelligence.* New York: Bantam Books.

Hattie, J. and Yates, G. C. R. (2014). *Visible Learning and the Science of How We Learn.* New York: Routledge.

Hicks, C., Glasgow, N., and McNary, S. (2004). *What Successful Mentors Do.* Thousand Oaks, CA: Corwin.

Holloway, J. (2001). The benefits of mentoring. *Educational Leadership* 58(8), 57–67.

Hyslop, A. (October 17, 2011). Harkin-Enzi ESEA Reauthorization 2.0 *The Quick and the Ed.* http://www.quickanded.com/2011/10/harkin-enzi-esea-reauthorization-2-0.html.

Jackson, Y., and McDermott, V. (2012). *Aim High, Achieve More: How to Transform Urban Schools through Fearless Leadership.* Alexandria, VA: ASCD.

John, P., and Gilchrist, I. (1999). Flying solo: Understanding the post-lesson dialogue between student teacher and mentor. *Mentoring and Tutoring* 7(2), 101–11.

Johnson, D., and Johnson, F. (2002). *Joining together* (8th edition). Boston: Allyn & Bacon.

Johnson-Bailey, J., and Cervero, R. (2004). Mentoring in black and white: The intricacies of cross-cultural mentoring. *Mentoring and Tutoring* 12(1), 7–21.

Kay, R. (1990). A definition for developing self-reliance. In T. Bey and C. Holmes (Eds.), *Mentoring: Developing Successful New Teachers.* Reston, VA: Association of Teacher Educators.

Kay, R. (1992). Mentor-management: Emphasizing the HUMAN in managing human resources. In T. Bey and C. Holmes (Eds.), *Mentoring: Contemporary principles and issues.* Reston, VA: Association of Teacher Educators.

Kersten, T. and Clauson, M. (2015). *Personnel Priorities in Schools Today.* Lanham, MD: Rowman & Littlefield.

Lasley, T. (1996). Mentors: They simply believe. *Peabody Journal of Education,* 71(1), 64–70.

Lindley, F. (2003). *The Portable Mentor.* Thousand Oaks, CA: Corwin.

Lipton, L., and Wellman, B. (September 2007). How to talk so teachers listen. *Educational Leadership* 65(1), 30–34.

Little, P. (2005). Peer coaching as a support to collaborative teaching. *Mentoring and Tutoring* 13(1), 83–94.

Manusov, V. (2009). Negative affect reciprocity. In H. T. Reis and S. K. Sprecher (Eds.), Encyclopedia of Human Relationships. Thousand Oaks, CA: Sage.

Manusov, V. (2005). *The Sourcebook of Nonverbal Measures: Going beyond Words.* Mahwah, NJ: Erlbaum.

Manusov, V., and Doohan, E. M. (2011). "My facial expression showed her that the woman could talk forever!": Meanings assigned to nonverbal cues used in relationships. In D. Chadee and A. Kostic (Eds.), Research in Social Psychology (69–92). Kingston, Jamaica: University of the West Indies Press.

Marshall, H. (1990). Metaphor as an instructional tool in encouraging student teacher reflection. *Theory Into Practice* 29(2), 128–32.

Marzano, R. (2007). *The Art and Science of Teaching.* Reston, VA: ASCD.

Marzano, R. (2013). *Scales and Evidence for the Marzano Teacher Evaluation Model.* Learning Sciences. www.marzanocenter.com.

Marzano, R., and Toth, M. (2013). *Teacher Evaluation That Makes a Difference.* Alexandria,VA: ASCD.

Maynard, T. (2000). Learning to teach or learning to manage mentors? Experiences of school-based teacher training. *Mentoring and Tutoring* 8(1), 17–30.

McEwan, E. K. (2003). *Ten Traits of Highly Effective Principals: From Good to Great Performance.* Thousand Oaks, CA: Sage.

Metts, S. (2000). Face and facework: Implications for the study of personal relationships. In K. Dindia and S. Duck (Eds.), *Communication and Personal Relationships.* Chichester, UK: Wiley.

Moir, E., and Bloom, G. (2003). Fostering leadership through mentoring. *Educational Leadership* 60(8), 58–60.

National Commission on Teaching and America's Future. (2000). NCRTL (National Center of Research on Teacher Learning) *Explores Learning from Mentors: A Study Update.* Retrieved July 29, 2005 fromhttp://www.educ.msu.edu/alumni/newed/ne66c3~5.htm.

Nye, B., et al., (Fall, 2004), How large are teacher effects? *Educational Evaluation and Policy Analysis* 26(3), 237–57.

Obidah, J., and Teel, K. (2000). *Because of the kids: Facing racial and cultural differences in schools.* New York: Teachers College Press.

Orland, L. (2005). Lost in translation: Mentors learning to participate in competing discources of practice. *Journal of Teacher Education* 56(4), 35–36.

Orland, L. (2000). Reading a mentoring situation: One aspect of learning to mentor. *Teaching and Teacher Education* 17(1), 75–88.

Pauker, R. and Hibbard, M. (2013). *Matching Your Message to the Audience. A Practical Guide to Structuring Language for New Administrators.* Lanham, MD: Rowman & Littlefield.

Peterson, B. (2004). *Cultural Intelligence: A Guide to Working with People from Other Cultures.* Yarmouth, ME: Intercultural Press.

Pitton, D. (2006). *Mentoring Novice Teachers: Fostering a Dialogue Process,* 2nd edition. Thousand Oaks, CA: Corwin Press.

Renard, L. (2003). Setting new teachers up for failure . . . or success. *Educational Leadership* 60(8), 62–64.

Rippon, J., and Martin, M. (2002). Supporting induction: Relationships count. *Mentoring and Tutoring* 11(2), 211–26.

Roberts, A. (2000). Mentoring revisited: A phenomenological reading of the literature. *Mentoring and Tutoring* 8(2), 145–70.

Rosenfeld, L. B. (1979). Self-disclosure avoidance: Why I am afraid to tell you who I am. *Communication Monographs* 46, 72–73.

Schon, D. (1990). *Educating the Reflective Practitioner.* San Francisco: Jossey-Bass.

Schubert, W., and Ayers, W. (1992). *Teacher Lore: Learning from Our Own Experience.* New York: Longman.

Shank, M. (2005). Mentoring among high school teachers: A dynamic and reciprocal group process. *Mentoring and Tutoring* 13(1), 73–82.

Shea, G. (1998). *Mentoring: How to Develop Successful Mentor Behaviors.* Menlo Park, CA: Crisp.

Sinclair, C. (2003). Mentoring online about mentoring: Possibilities and practice. *Mentoring and Tutoring* 11(1), 79–95.

Smith, J. (2005). Understanding the beliefs, concerns and priorities of trainee teachers: A multidisciplinary approach. *Mentoring and Tutoring* 13(2), 205–19.Stanulis, R., Fallona, C. and Pearson, C. (2002) Are we doing what we are supposed to be doing? Mentoring novices through the uncertainties and challenges of their first year of teaching. *Mentoring and Teaching* 10(1), 71–81.

Stanulis, R., and Manning, B. H. (2002). The teacher's role in creating a positive verbal and nonverbal environment. *Early Childhood Education Journal* 30(1), 3–8.

Stanulis, R., and Russell, D. (2000). Jumping in: Trust and communication in mentoring student teachers. *Teaching and Teacher Education: An International Journal of Research and Studies* 16(1), 65–80.

Storms, B., Wing, J., et al. (2000). *CFASST* (California Formative Assessment and Support System) (field review) *implementation 1999–2000: A Formative Evaluation Report.* Princeton, NJ: Educational Testing Service.

Tatum, B., McWhorter, P., et al., (1999). Maybe not everything, but a whole lot you always wanted to know about mentoring. In P. Graham, S. Hudson-Ross, C. Adkins, P. McWhorter and J. Stewart (Eds.), *Teacher/Mentor* (21–34). New York: Teachers College Press.

Thomas, D. (2001). The truth about mentoring minorities: Race matters. *Harvard Business Review* 79(4), 98–107.

Trager, G. (1958). Paralanguage: A first approximation. *Studies in Linguistics* 13, 1–12.

Wallace, J. (1999). The dialogue journal. In P. Graham, S. Hudson-Ross, C. Adkins, P. McWhorter, J. Stewart (Eds.), *Teacher/Mentor.* New York: Teachers College Press.

Young, J., Alvermann D., Kaste, J., Henderson, S., and Many, J. (2004). Being a friend and a mentor at the same time: A pooled case comparison. *Mentoring and Tutoring* 12(1), 24–36.

Van Der Valk, A. (June 9, 2015). Under Attack. *Teaching Tolerance.* Montgomery, AL: Southern Poverty Law Center. tolerance@Splcmail.org, 50–52.

Zachary, L. (2000). *The Mentor's Guide: Facilitating Effective Learning Relationships.* San Francisco: Jossey Bass.

Zull, J. (2002) *The Art of Changing the Brain.* Sterling, VA: Stylus Publishing.

Index

111

Scales and Evidence for the Marzano Teacher Evaluation Model, 44, 48–52, 50

scripting, 75; example of notes in, 74; formats for data, 69–72, 74; post-observation conference and, 71–72; techniques for honing principals', 72

signals, mixed, 26. *See also* checking signals

skills, strengthening communication, 101

stereotypes, 13

strategies, teaching, 19

structure, 99; funding, mentors and, 94, 94–95; teacher evaluation success and, 94–95

students, 106; classroom observations and engagement of, 63, 66–69, 102, 104; distractions for, 76; favoritism of, 105; mentoring responses for assessing, 102; mentoring responses for disruptive, 103, 104; mentoring responses for engagement of, 102, 104; mentoring responses for feedback to, 104; mentoring responses for motivating, 103; mentoring responses for struggling, 105; numeric evidence for behavior of, 76–77

success: confidentiality for teacher learning, 93–94; principals developing structures for, 94–95; resources and practices for, 93–99; structure and funding for teacher evaluations, 94–95

support, reflection and principals', 85. *See also* teacher support

surveys, mentoring response exercise for, 106

taking turns aspect, of nonverbal communication, 36–37

teacher evaluations: access of instructional resources for, 98–99; confidentiality of personnel files and, 24; conversation guidelines and confidentiality in, 23–24; creation of time allowances for, 97–98; data and processes for, 96–97, 99; feedback and, 24–25, 84; identifying rationale for, 96–97; implementation of updated, 4; principals' guidance for success of,

93–99; relationships and difficult, 5, 5–6; strengthening skills for, 101–106; structure and funding for, 94–95; support for teachers' weaknesses in, 60–61; systems and tools for, 1–2; time concerns for, 97–98; trust as key in environment of, 11–13. *See also* evaluation tools; *The Framework for Teaching Evaluation Instrument*; *The Marzano Teacher Evaluation Model*; *Scales and Evidence for the Marzano Teacher Evaluation Model*

teacher learning: confidentiality for success in, 93–94; creating environment to support, 11–20; data gathering and rationales for, 63–78; goal setting for development and, 81–90; goal setting for expanding, 86–87; numeric evidence and, 77; positive interactions and trust in, 11–13; post-observation conference data for, 64–65; post-observation questions for, 70–71, 84; questioning process for support of, 55–61, 84; videos and audiotaping in classrooms for, 78

teachers, 102–103; clarification of verbal messages and, 28–29; evaluation tool selection for principals and, 52–53; evaluation tools for development of, 41–53; evaluation tools for work evidence of, 44–53; evaluation weaknesses and support for, 60–61; feedback and evaluations of, 24–25, 84; guidance questions for, 82, 83–85; lens as evaluation tools for, 41–43, 43–45, 49–53; mentoring expectations for, 8–9; mentoring for errors of, 105; mentoring for lesson planning of, 103; modeling strategies of, 19; movement indicators and observations of, 75, 76; post-observation goals and roles of, 64–65; principals mentoring and role of, 5–6, 16; principals understanding views of, 18–19; reflection options by principals and, 86. *See also* principal/teacher role-playing

teacher support: post-observation as component of, 61; questioning process for learning and, 55–61, 84; weaknesses

About the Author

Dr. Debra Eckerman Pitton taught high school and middle-level language arts and theater and speech, worked as assistant superintendent for curriculum and learning, and served as an elected member of her local school board. Debra completed her PhD in curriculum and instruction at the University of North Texas and is currently on the faculty of Gustavus Adolphus College in St. Peter, Minnesota.

Debra's focus is teaching secondary and middle-level methods and international service learning courses. She also chairs the education department and supervises student teachers. She has worked with districts across the country to help teachers and educational leaders develop mentoring and teacher support skills. She lives in Burnsville, Minnesota, with her husband, Jon, and has three adult children.